THE CHRONICLES OF
BARGEPOLE

Michael Bywater hasn't had a proper job since 1979, but nevertheless has managed to have a really good time. As well as a freelance journalist, he's a qualified commercial pilot, photographer, harpsichordist, failed doctor and red-hot lover. He is also much sought after by the tax authorities on three continents. Additionally, he is a reluctant computer guru, an occasional TV presenter, and once wrote a film which was hailed by the critics as 'even worse than *Banger Boys*'.

He has one daughter, lives in Bloomsbury with a bad yellow-eyed woman, and his marital status is *sub judice*.

THE CHRONICLES OF
BARGEPOLE

The Man Who Wouldn't Be Gagged

Michael Bywater

PICADOR

IN ASSOCIATION WITH JONATHAN CAPE

For Isabella, Anita, Marlene, Helen,
Georgiana, Agneta, Kate, Susan, Celine,
Amanda and Chen, who drove me to it.

And for Benedicta, who didn't.

First published 1992 by Jonathan Cape Limited

This Picador edition published 1993 by Pan Books Limited
a division of Pan Macmillan Publishers Limited
Cavaye Place London SW10 9PG
and Basingstoke

in association with Jonathan Cape Limited

Associated companies throughout the world

ISBN 0 330 32880 8

The pieces published here first appeared in *Punch*

1 3 5 7 9 8 6 4 2

A CIP catalogue record for this book is available from
the British Library

Printed and bound in Great Britain by
Cox & Wyman Ltd, Reading, Berkshire

INTRODUCTION

BARGEPOLE WAS BORN in the mid–Eighties, just as the monstrous outbreak of consumerism was beginning to engulf us all like . . . well, like a monstrous out-break of consumerism. There are enough metaphors to come, without clogging up the introduction as well.

I found myself ahead of the fashion. I had already had my own m. o. of c. in the early Eighties, culminating in the purchase of an aeroplane, and now the air was heavy with the cries of chickens coming home to roost. I was, in short, in a fine position to comment on the insanity of unfettered materialism.

Punch, on the other hand, was having to face the fact that the world had changed irrevocably. In one of those astounding management insights for which management is celebrated, we were handed a thick wad of demographics and market research, and told to appeal to the Reader's interests.

Before they gave us all the statistics, we had little idea of what the Reader's interests were. But after ploughing through the turgid wad of trivia and half-truth, we had *no idea whatsoever*. We no longer even knew who the Reader was.

Nevertheless I was sent off to start a new section at the back of *Punch*, appealing to his interests. I tried every-thing: museums, tobacco, briefcases, cake, fish, rubberwear, skydiving – the lot.

Before long, I began to hate the Reader and all his interests. This was no everyday pique, but a fine and generous loathing: I hated *everything*, on the off-chance that it might turn out to be something the Reader liked.

Most of all, I hated the press releases. Since we were now publishing 'consumer-oriented features' the press releases came flooding in, an inundation of paper so staggeringly, mind-bendingly fatuous, self-regarding and nakedly venal that our eyes began to bubble and didn't stop until, mercifully, the recession kicked in just in time.

One press release in particular stays in my mind. It showed a picture of a sniggering, porky bozo in a cheap suit who had been appointed to some post or other in a computer company. I ranted for a while about this to Alan Coren, then the editor of *Punch*, who crept off and wrote a little piece about a different sort of bugger: some fat pimp picking his conk in a Rolls-Royce Corniche.

Alan's piece was so horrible that we all took the decision not only not to publish it, but to destroy the manuscript and never mention it, ever again.

But from this vile beginning, Bargepole was born. The name came from the column's subject matter, which was all the stuff you wouldn't want to touch with one. Alan believes that *he* thought up the name, and I believe that *I* did, an honest difference of recollection in which he is wrong and I am right. I got to write Bargepole, while poor Alan had to content himself with editorships, columns in *The Times*, a Mercedes, a house in Provence and all the rest of the material consolations God hands out to those who never manage quite to hit life on the sweet spot.

At first, we wondered how They would take it. The traditional English type of comic writing depends on the writer claiming kinship with his readers in gently mocking those national institutions in which we all believe. But by the mid-Eighties, there were no such institutions.

Gentle satire, too, was no longer enough, something brought home to me when I received a press release announcing a meeting, to be held by a well-known London council, to discuss the particular problems of disabled black lesbians. *I am not making this up*.

I went along. It was a grey, damp, cheerless evening of the sort which will always mean home to those who hate England. Outside the dirty brick building, three bedraggled

2

thirty-ish women, badly knitted out of home-grown muesli, stood by a hand-scrawled notice saying METING ON 3D FL. *There were no disabled black lesbians* . . . which was a good thing, since there was also no wheelchair ramp or lift; how could they have got into the building and up to the 3D FL?

So satire was out. There was no point, now that people were on the streets doing it for real. And the old posture of lovably humorous incompetence was simply inappropriate while the country was being overrun by Killer Dorks From Planet Sprod.

So what we gave the readers instead was what you will see in the following pages. Strangely, they loved it. Even more strangely, the women *really* loved it.

I guess, in general, Bargepole caught a small but responsive nerve. We were in transit between a decade where everyone was supposed to be mean, hard-headed and governed by the profit motive, and another decade when we were all supposed to become sensitive, caring, egalitarian and at one with nature. The truth is that both postures were, are and always will be largely irrelevant to most of us, and are a lot of cock got up by dim journalists anxious to fill the pages. As the late Myles nà gCopaleen said, 'Give a man plenty of food, beer and the chance to score off his enemies, and you won't hear much whining out of *him*.' It's a line I've been passing off as my own ever since.

And that, if you like, is the continuing theme of Bargepole, who is continually startled and enraged by the fact that we are being conned into thinking irrelevancies are significant. TV personalities, jerk politicians, spanner-faced businessmen, liars, bores and gaseously inflated self-elected honchos of every kidney are all trying to make us *do* something, *think* something, *pay for* something . . . and we don't give a damn about it all. Not about the rain forests, nor about Maastricht, the Yen, Jason Donovan's preferred recreational orifice, the snivelling, affronted little git from American Express . . . *none of it matters*.

3

Not even, God help us, the problems of disabled black lesbians.

Which is what Bargepole pointed out. The men seemed to like it, but the women went a stage further, and used to send him letters, the kind you'd have to put out on the windowledge to cool. Everything women were *telling* men suggested that a character like Bargepole would be purest anathema, but here they were, squirming over the bugger . . . and there's a lesson there. It's this: the worst way in which a man can try to please a woman is by trying to please her, and I offer that free to all those sad, confused men out there writing books about coming to terms with post-feminism. Post-feminism can come to terms with *us*, or it'll only have itself to blame when it finds itself alone and crying in the middle of the night.

Bargepole died as he had lived. When the excitingly dynamic management of United Newspapers closed *Punch* without warning I filed the last Bargepole column from Hinton-in-the-Hedges airfield, where I was prosecuting some inquiries involving a slender brunette, a zebra finch and a second-hand aircraft. I left his last sentence unfinished, by way of a . . . well, a *joke*.

About an hour later, I got a call from the production editor. She was seriously clenched up. 'This piece', she said, 'is incomplete.'

There you go, then.

4

I

THE CREDITORS, SNIVELLING hounds, have risen from the ground again, bubbling and dripping and snarling for my blood. The air is thick like snow again with writs, threats, affidavits and all the rest of the drivelling paraphernalia upon which the lawyers (yellow teeth, scum at the corners of the mouth, thin wives with wiry pubic hair) thrive, or believe themselves to be thriving. My own lawyer is currently in a South American jail owing to a piece of bad luck involving a Gulfstream jet, a bottle of mezcal and a jungle, so I am on my own.

I suppose I should feel miserable and afraid but I cannot seem to work up the enthusiasm. People look at me as though I should behave like a whipped dog but I am inclined to tough it out. The only problem is that They Won't Like Me Any More, but they don't like me anyway so that isn't a problem. There is only one I remotely care about, and a little criminal activity will soon take care of *that*, and the rest can go hang. Who can possibly wish anything but the most cataclysmic and nightmarish evil upon the reeking, timid, monosyllabic cravens of American Express, or the polyester-clad premature ejaculators from the Inland Revenue? Not me, anyway: I may be a good Catholic, but I am not fanatical, and when it comes to sexual continence or forgiveness of enemies, Holy Mother Church and I must agree to differ.

But I do wonder why most of us carry on. The woman I used to love (I went off her quite suddenly last Monday, in my blameless bath) said she envied what she chose to call my life. 'It must be lovely,' she said, 'writing what you want, when you want, not having to answer to anyone; it's really rather impressive.' Silly tart. What does she know? She spends her life being psychotically vicious to people she is supposed to placate and flatter. I, on the other hand, am *paid*

5

to be horrible, and there's nobody I'm supposed to grease up to, so where's the fun in that? She gets the money and the fast car and the fun of it being bad to be horrid, and all I get is grief and writs, and the agony of forcing out scabrous abuse when all I really want to do is live in a little room somewhere and write books about love and truth.

And beauty? You can stuff beauty up your finely tuned burbling exhaust, it being nothing but a snare and a curse. Call me an unregenerate Big-Ears if you will, but I am beyond all that now. I spent the evening in a beastly night-club again, and I'm not going any more, because all the women in their short skirts excited neither my amatory propensities nor any other propensities. You wouldn't want to talk to them. It would be like eating Andrex. And once you've decided that you don't want to poke them, there is no point in impressing them.

The sense of liberation in no longer wanting to impress the bastards is astounding. The ones who are worth impressing are the ones who wouldn't be impressed if you impressed them, and immediately the road to freedom lies ahead, in plain view.

Do you see what I mean? It's the damned Y-chromosome. One sees a perfect figure in a grey jersey Alaïa frockette, and one thinks 'I want a go on that,' but the truth is that one has been duped by the frock and the gold jewellery and the fancy barnet and the Porsche . . . and it's all impossibly reflexive. They sport the frock, jewels, cars and barnets in order to get the sort of men who will buy them more frocks, jewels, cars and barnets, so that they – what? I mean, *what*? Such a lot of miserable carping buggers they are, but how about the poor men? Might as well wear the frocks, jewels and barnets themselves, then at least they'd only have to buy one set. As it is, it's keep them coming or get dumped, and the things you have to do to provide that stuff. Merciful heavens, you'd have to work in PR or the rock business or advertising or maybe even, if you were intellectually challenged and barking mad, be a fashionable society lawyer.

6

All awful things, you will agree. So awful, in fact, that the only solace available is in taking expensive women home in Porsches, removing their frocks and jewels, and sodding up their barnets.

Take away the Y-chromosome, free yourself from the yelping testosterone imperative, and the chains of slavery are immediately broken. Not only do you not need 'people' like that, but you don't even *want* them, and can do as you like. You can stop shaving, run to seed, inhabit just as much space on the planet as you require and no more, and get on with doing what you like best, which in my case is writing stuff, playing Frescobaldi, taking pictures and flying around the place. When you have spent so much time flying that you haven't written anything to pay for it, you simply go bankrupt again, and since you aren't trying to impress anyone it doesn't matter: far from failing, you have succeeded in doing precisely what you want, without falling victim to the delusion that other people's opinion of you is more important than having a good time.

Try an experiment. What exactly do you possess or strive to possess *solely to give yourself pleasure*? In my case, it's (a) my uncle's old Rolex, (b) my harpsichord, (c) my Leicas and (d) a few books of which I am particularly fond. Everything else is, to a greater or lesser extent, there to impress. And who do I want to impress? Not men. No time for them. Men are full of dogshit. No: it's *women* I want to impress. And why should that be? So that they'll go to bed with me.

Well: enough of that. From now on, anyone who needs to be impressed before they will go to bed with me will simply have to forego one of the most powerful, moving and indeed almost hypnotically terrifying things that can happen to a woman. The Inland Revenue and American Express can do their worst. Bankers, accountants and lawyers can whistle for their tainted gold. It's Big-Ears time for me, boys, and if any of you want to join me in this exciting insouciant wonderland, just pop round and I'll lop your balls off with one swipe of my pruning knife, providing it hasn't been seized by the bailiffs first.

2

THIS IS WHAT will happen: I shall one night forget to fill reservoir (2), press button (6) and turn valve (3) anti-clockwise, but will leave switch (9) pressed. The boiler will not refill. There will be a smell of hot metal as I twitch and shrivel in my bed, the slow-weld reek which haunts my dreaming and waking alike, but I shall ignore it.

In the morning, I shall, in accordance with the instructions, depress button (6): I shall tell it that I cannot become the sort of person it wants me to become and if it hopes for any sort of relationship with me, it will get hurt. If that doesn't depress it, I shall tell it there is no God. There will be a blast of superheated plasma and stinking aluminium, and that will be that. The last thing will have gone.

It's a pity. The cappuccino machine was quite a nice last thing to have, even though it doesn't play a major role in the eschatology of the Magisterium. I suppose something had to go; death, judgement, heaven, hell and cappuccino were just too many variables for even the theological mind to play with at once. Personally I would have struck out death, but then the rest would have been redundant: on the other hand, how many people's lives have been enriched by eschatology? If you look carefully, women aren't in there either, but then they aren't really last things. At least, I've never met one who lasted. They're more penultimate, really, and they know it: they are just about the last straw but somehow one keeps coming back for more, or, in my case, for less.

I suppose the reason women don't figure much in formal theology is because they compete with God. Both are figments of our imagination. We delude ourselves into thinking that we will one day find a woman who loves us and that God loves us all the time, anyway, but it's balls and it's beside the point. What we really want is some woman to welcome our love and be glad that it's offered, and when they say things like 'I'm not going to change, I can't give you what you want, I really don't want to lose you but on the other hand I don't give a fuck,' we invent God, just so that there's someone there pleading away for us to love Him.

So that's that one gone. The harpsichord went, too. I was giving it a bit of a tuning – A 415 Hz, if you must know, Bach temperament – and tenor C went bang, and a couple of jacks snapped, and then entropy really got its claws in, plectra breaking off, key-leathers unpeeling and the 4-foot sliding steadily downwards towards A = 0 Hz as ineluctably as a junket down a well-greased invalid ramp.

The only reason I had been tuning it at all was that God was supposed to be coming round for dinner, or it may have been a woman. A woman coming round for dinner, I mean, not God coming round for a woman, twice in two thousand years would be pushing it a bit, one feels. I had it all laid out nicely: spot of Bach to set the mood, dish of snails, something dead with truffles up it, and then one of those useful three-bottle conversations which end up in bed or tears, except she forgot and when I rang up she went for the jugular. You are pathetic, you are trying to manipulate me, I warned you at the beginning, I cannot make a commitment, I really really don't want to lose you.

Bah, and humbug. Commitment? Committal would be appropriate and as for *I don't want to lose you* just try finding me now, tucked up snug on the eschatology page here. So I ate the snails alone, and was sick, and ran around the house shouting, and now I have gone off her and God and Bach and snails and the harpsichord and I don't like it here because I sit on my bum trying to finish this tackily vicious smart-arse London novel and I don't like the novel either. I've gone off my clothes because I never go anywhere to wear them because I've nobody to go with and anyway I sit here writing the tacky novel, and I've gone off my camera because it broke and there's only the cappuccino machine to go.

There was the dog, of course; always the dog.

But the dog is dead, now. Bitch. We bought her when I was happy with somebody – I know I was happy because I wrote it down in my little notebook – and we took her for long walks in Burnham Beeches and then somebody stole her and abused her and she was never the same after that. Became a mad dog, incapable of trust, suspicious, had to sleep alone, snarled through her muzzle, attacked those who loved her and earlier this week she went too far and the woman I was once happy with took her up to Burnham Beeches and had the *quietus* gently administered and buried her where she used to run.

I had a bit of a cry, but whether it was sadness, empathy or envy, I can't tell. Perhaps we invented death just like we invented God and women: when I lie in my silly big bed with the other side littered with books, manuscripts, Leica, bottle of lighter fuel, spare spare rib, bottle of Laphroaig, bag of peppermints, TV remote control, old contact sheets, cheque book, stuffed dog with label saying 'I Love You Because . . .' but not filled in, then I think, Yes, we did. Proved about as useful as the Sinclair C5, too.

Perhaps I should do something with the spare rib, but niche marketing is where the opportunities lie these days. The dog has gone and I've been reading Stevie Smith, been too far out all my life, and not waving but drowning. Oh yes? Pourquoi pas en profiter, then? There are plenty in that position. We have Knicker Box and Tie Rack so why not Snuff Shop, strategic sites wherever misery thrives, pop in off the street, hand over the credit card and we put you down, returning your remains to your loved ones in a smart box with a nice environmental logotype. Your problem is to think of any loved ones, and the pain of that confrontation might just push you over the brink. And *my* problem? I don't have a problem. I will get rich. Nothing else counts. First thing I'll do is buy myself a God.

3

THE THING ABOUT asymptomatic influenza is that nobody believes you've got it. They may be right and
perhaps you haven't, but I have. Still. Can't get up
but on the other hand can't sleep, just lie there contemplating
suicide but without the get-up-and-go to top myself. The Da
says it's just the virus. As if that helps. I thought of ringing
the Samaritans, but can you imagine what they would be
like? Awful people in woollen jerseys who *want to help*. Five
minutes of being understood at by one of those bloody men
who respects his wife as a human being ('No, no: let Candida
have her say') and I would have been violently angry as well as
plunged into an iridescent kind of despair, life as an abattoir,
eternity as a Pitte, love as a sort of lethal glue, and then I would
have had to get up.

I did not want to get up. It would probably have done
me the world of good but I wasn't prepared to do it because
of the insomnia: after days of squelching sadly around my
basket, hallucinating lethally and fighting with the sheets, I
went out and spent hundreds and hundreds of pounds on
new bed, bedlinen, and Thing. You know: a muesli. The
muesli alone was £250 and stuffed with goose-down. Years
ago we didn't have mueslis, just blankets, and then suddenly
they caught on: how odd that there was all that goose-down
to meet the demand, I said to the woman in the shop, but she
said, No, the cheaper ones are duck, and if you think about it
the fashion for Chinese food preceded the fashion for Things,
they were chopping up duck from Peking to the Himalayas
and saving all the feathers, the clever little buggers.

But I still couldn't sleep. It was very comfortable but
there's a limit to how long you can lie there thinking
'This is very comfortable,' and after the unalloyed triumph
of Old Girlfriends' Week (mind your own business) I found

myself condemned to a hateful solitude, contemplating my memories, most of which I seemed to have forgotten. I was just about to get up when I stopped breathing. When I was a medical student we were taught that this is one of the symptoms of what doctors call 'death'. Not just doctors: locums do, too, when the doctors are on holiday having a bit of a ski, something a bit energetic up Gstaad, bend from the hips, weight on the outside edge, go with the curves, watch the rhythm and make sure she has her orgasm first.

I've never heard such rubbish in my life. How can you tell? They made me see that film the other day, *When What's-his-name Met What's-her-name*, the one where she has one in the delicatessen, and all the men in the cinema winced and looked sheepish. Not me. I found it utterly unconvincing. Nobody has *ever* made noises like that in my presence, and if they did I'd throw them out fast. Pure histrionics, if you discount the possibility that the women in my past could not even be bothered to fake it properly, which is of course ludicrous: we harpsichordists are known to be the world's finest lovers, possessing all the necessary skills: a precise, quick but featherlight touch, a bone-cracking sense of tempo and rhythm, the ability to light a cigarette with one hand while playing *Pralltriller* with the other, and a little bag containing a hammer, a tuning fork, a pair of pliers and a length of copper wire.

Add to that an iron lung, if the breathing problem comes back. It was only half the process which went wrong, the breathing out part. I could suck the stuff in but getting rid of it again was impossible, so I lay there thinking 'This is comfortable but not as comfortable as it was' and wondering if an untipped Camel, lightly smoked, would unbung the works, and waiting for my life to flash past. I waited and waited and finally realised it *had* flashed past already, over the last 35 years. Nobody ever told me it did it in real time, so the only thing to do was get up.

I thought at first a spot of work would help but there was a kebab in my top left hand drawer so I went out to a club of which I am not a member (there are hundreds like that, so no shortage of choice) and sat there with a face like a stuck pig drinking gin-and-ginger and talking in a desultory fashion to a chap who must have had bladder flu: he kept going off to the lavatory and coming back with a runny nose, talking very fast. Then someone else turned up and said, 'You'll have to go away, I'm meeting this chap and he hates you because you are young and vigorous,' so I gave a short bark of laughter which got rid of some of the excess breath and stayed put and he turned up and we got on like David and Jonathan (both dead). Which would have been all very well except he then decided to put in a good word for me with someone I want to write for and someone I want a favour from and a woman I want to go to bed with so I've really had it.

The thing to do is to be gay. We decided that in order to succeed with women you have to be a rich, nasty dickhead. Rich because that's what they like; nasty because it makes them think you're going to go on being rich; and a dickhead because only a dickhead would think it's worth being nasty to be rich. Gays don't have these problems although they do have others which we can hardly even imagine, although in California it's a different story: choreography has changed for ever and you can't get a decent haircut anywhere in LA, according to that awful man, what's his name, who should be shot.

I was thinking about this when I read that the *Tatler* 'stylist', a gorgeously venomous mincing boogie known as Michael Roberts, otherwise known as the African Queen, has buggered off. The Inland Revenue wanted to make him bankrupt so he just vanished. Poof! he was gone, and could afford to, owning no possessions, bound by no hopeless yearnings, no question of 'What will she think?' or 'I'll never see her again,' or 'What about the alimony?' It's an example I would like to follow, but where do you go to be made gay? My mother has her hands full at the moment and anyway missed her chance, and would anyone else's mother do the trick? I wouldn't have thought so.

14

I SHALL BE staying in this time. The feast of St Valentine will pass me by. The nasty jangling little time-bombs of self-regard and betrayal can stay unpublished, nor will the greetings-card industry have any fiscal assistance from me. There is so little point in bothering.

I suppose this means that I have lost a grip on the *Zeitgeist* but who cares about the *Zeitgeist* anyway? The only interesting thing about it is that we don't have our own word for it, though oddly enough we seem more obsessed with it than any other nation on earth. I have had to read a number of women's magazines lately and they all seem obsessed with the notion that life is about being different today than you were yesterday.

They are wrong, of course. Life is all about deciding who you are and staying like it, even if you are wrong, but that won't do for the women's magazines. Oh no. You have to overturn your life, change your wardrobe, paint your face differently, shed your job, dump your man, lose unsightly fat, liberate yourself from the misery of painful periods, learn from others, share your experiences, face reality, take control of your relationships, buy a new car and learn how to show yards of slim, five-denier leg as you get out of it outside the Soho Brasserie to have dinner with a man in a slightly dated, black Armani suit who is, O my *gawd*, even wittier than John Sessions, never mind the sheer scrumptious mouth-watering, everythingelse-watering hunky *yumminess* of (*insert name of skilfully marketed showbiz personality*) and a schlong like a stovepipe.

This is the Dream of the Nineties, and what you will do, girlies, is pair-bond. There's you with your reconstructed half-consciousness, and there's him with his subtly potent range of toiletries. I see (*rubs crystal ball, peers in, sees reflection of grey, puffy face, recoils*) you going back to His Place which of course is decorated in perfect taste. I see you smiling to yourself as you observe the wittily rococo decor. Pickled pitchpine, frescos, gilded gesso, bloody grapes and fruit everywhere. His spinet stands in a corner and apsley yards and yards of raw silk drape the Napoleonic daybed standing by the bonsai baobab from which Chatterton, a raven, taunts the two grey Persian cats circling beneath. A decanter of madeira – I was going to say mead, but I thought, fuck it – is decorously sipped from those nasty greenish glasses with the odd bubble in them because, frankly, they weren't much good at making glasses in those days. A little Orlando Lassus is . . . no, whoops, a little Monteverdi, the better class of Monteverdi, *Il Combattimento*, perhaps, is dispensed from the . . . no, what is dispensed from the gramophone (concealed behind a trompe l'oeil screen) is Handel. *The Triumph of Time and Truth*. The first version of 1703 if I'm not much mistaken, note the sublime sensuality and yet incorruptible purity of the pending trill on the last aria, life is . . . delicate and fine and yet . . . alone it all seems somehow so, so, oh I don't know, my sweet, it's just that when we met I simply realised that we pass through the world alone and our only chance of salvation is to make that . . . one might almost say that transcendent and miraculous *connection* with another human being, yes, yes, I speak of marriage, a celebration of our lives entwinéd, children running at one's feet, one does so see oneself as, oh, I don't know, one of those dickheads in a floppy hat out of a Flemish interior, say you will be mine my darling and, together, we will wave ta-ta to the tacky solipsism of the Eighties and welcome in a new era of black-and-white floor tiles, fidelity, and transcendent peace.

And now (*starts to rub ball again, remembers, stops*) I see a decorous but impassioned courtship take place. He bends over you: honeyed breath, eyes clear, something writhing in his irreproachable breeks like two frogs in a washcloth. Perhaps he bites into a ripe peach. You stretch languorously; he, overwhelmed by the promise of your acquiescence, carries

16

you off to his bedroom. Who knows, the floor may even be strewn with rushes but they will be *fresh* rushes, changed once a week by the nice young man from Justin de Blank . . . and he lays you down on the heavy linen sheets and gazes into your eyes and says: No . . . not now . . . not yet . . . I want it to be . . . *perfect*; when I make love to you I want it to be as man and wife, but, by the way, I have my own business, £150,000 a year and the house is paid for.

This is the Nineties. This is what it is going to be like. Elegant, civilised, monogamous. What a lucky little bimbette you are. Now you can leave that awful job. No need to elbow the men aside. No need to crush your feet into stilettos any longer. Throw away your Rifat Ozbek, pippit, and check into perpetual connubiality, your eyes full of babies. Happiness is striding up over the brow of the hill in its nice shoes and its velvet cloak, whistling *The Sun Has Got His Hat On* and you can stop *thinking*, stop *striving*, the heat is off, the pressure is off, all that self-obsessed status-definition is now just passé.

But who knows, really? Who are the people who *know the truth about what you are like and what it is like*? Yes: the people who do the advertisements. And have you looked at *those*? Have you noticed, darling, how, with your glossy hair and your slim figure, your control and equipoise, your GTi Turbo Convertible and your designer water . . . have you noticed, chickadee, that you are *alone*? With your cat? Sometimes with your bicycle or your hi-fi system, sometimes with your car, sometimes with your Rolleiflex, sometimes with your espresso, but always *alone*?

So it's going to be an interesting decade, an interesting year, and an interesting week. Cut out the Valentines and keep them: next year may be very different: *Is there anyone out there who would like to be called Mister Toad? Luv, your Snugglebums.*

5

FROM TIME TO TIME I find myself in Clubs. Sometimes gentlemen's clubs, sometimes nightclubs. 'A victory for new Britain over old Britain'? Good God no. Both are definitely Old.

They are old because the men who go there are no longer young. Gentlemen's clubs are full of men trying to make themselves feel younger than they are by pretending to be older than they are. Nightclubs are full of men trying to pull off the same trick by feeding cold champagne to cold young women in the hope of dancing with them, nuzzling them, then taking them off for a poke. Prolepsis made flesh.

Both are unsatisfactory but I suppose the primary difference is hope. Nightclub Man still clings to the hope that one day he will meet the one who will make it all worthwhile. He won't. The juicy baptism of a bimbo's loins cannot sanctify the unlovely struggle for power and money which has destroyed Nightclub Man. There's the vicious trap which springs too late: Nightclub Man wants the power and the money so that he can be part of the Nightclub set of men who are part of the Nightclub set because they've got the power and the money because *then* . . . *then* he can meet the sort of girls who go around with the sort of men who are part of the Nightclub set . . . No other reason. *These girls poke Eurotrash*: they will never, *ever* love him for himself.

But still he struts, he nuzzles, he settles the bill. His suit is Cerutti but his eyes are scared and when he tells her he loves her she thinks: sentimental: how I wish he would stop. He introduces her to his rich and influential friends: M&A specialists, shifty entrepreneurs, fringe-aristo lawyers, sallow poseurs with Bentleys and drivers because they know that Rolls-Royces and chauffeurs are common. She smiles and he thinks: which one will steal her?

18

Later, if there is a later, he wonders whether she will think less of him if he sucks in his little paunch or not. His platinum wristwatch scratches her buttock and her sighing and melting seems no different to him than all the other sighings and meltings he has pinned to the bed, but neither complains: two vampires, trained to the task: vampires stripped of the rumours of monstrosity are small and frail; their flight is clumsy; blind, they struggle in the dark and cry to find their way.

Failure after failure, ignominy after rejection after hateful revelation, they continue to hope. The going limp. The going off with the chap he introduced her to (more money, bigger car, more power, more influence, bigger dining-room, smarter address). The going round to her flat and finding her in bed tangled up close with some 26-year-old *penniless* swine *actor* (more muscles, more hair, more soul, more *interesting* darling more in *common* darling you *do* understand darling it's been such *fun* but it couldn't *last* darling you must have known that darling but darling I'll *always* treasure the mink and the *lovely lovely lovely* emerald collar darling darling) when she never curled up with *him* but slept lightly on the far side of the bed.

Hope: the devil's gift: poor carrion hope that makes humanity contemptible. Hope: all they seek in the end is love: intimacy, commitment, preference. But to hell with them. They have career plans and dimmer switches, self-regard, dinner parties; tell lies, boast, spend and trample, shout in the night; their souls are barnacled like hobnail livers; frequently they have enlarged pores and precarious voices; the remote control for the CD lives under the pillow (mood is *so* important).

In the Gentlemen's Club, things are different. Hope? Good God no. So *striving*. No no. Decent food. Spot of Burgundy. Pictures on the wall. Look. That one's a Zoffany, rather good, don't you think? So they say. Personally, I know a lot about art but I don't know what I like. Ha! Ha! Comfortable here, under the stairs, by the fire. I remember the evening when old Father Tendentious from Farm Street set his soutane on fire, wonderful chap, did you know him? Died, of course. Have I seen who? Oh yes. Rather unsuitable, I'd say, half his age, making a fool of himself, wife's frightfully nice and the soul of discretion but he's a bit of a laughing-stock. Terrible chap, turned up in new clothes with a Porsche . . . blackballed? Pure caviar, my dear fellow, not a glimmer of white to be seen when we looked in the box.

To be frank, I'd prefer to be Eurotrash, Nightclub Man: give me the big car, the hired man, the shifty occupation, the dodgy honorific, the Gold Card any day. Perhaps it seems odd to you. Being a member of neither sort of place nor ever likely to be; having no money, no power, no status; able to intimidate and boss nobody at all: why, surely I enjoy the greatest gift of all: knowing that I am loved for myself? Well, nuts. The fact is that nobody really gives a toss about me, just like nobody really gives a toss about you either. Trust? Intimacy? Bodies and souls merging as one? Pure fantasy. You might as well believe in Noddy, and while you're at it you might as well be rich and drink a lot and take cocaine and hang out with Nightclub Men and boff a lot of bright sparkling Azzedine Alaïa bimbos-on-the-make.

The only thing that bothers me about this entire strange episode is the prostitute stuff. Everybody seems anxious to prove that they hadn't a clue that Miss Bordes was a prostitute. Why? What is wrong with going around with prostitutes? I frequently go around with a prostitute and have done for years: I am extremely fond of her and she is a fund of excellent stories which I keep to myself; and if it was suggested by my enemies that I *knew* she was a prostitute, I would have to say: yes, one does need at least *one* honest friend.

Sue for damages? I wouldn't dream of it. Nor would that other chap. What was his name? Went around with a hooker; very fond of her; quite open about it. Oh, ages ago. Started a religion; you know the one I mean.

6

I HAVE DECIDED to become a homosexual. But how is it done? I don't mean the mechanics of it all; that is clear enough. Although I failed Anatomy Part I several times, I still know what's what and how a hiatus hernia operates. No, it's the other stuff. Fancying men, I mean. If it wasn't for that, I'd have become one long ago, in and out of the closet before you could say Hello, haven't seen you around here before.

It would have been easy enough in the old days. I had lunch with a man a few years ago and we were talking about San Francisco, where both he and I had spent some time before the . . . *unpleasantness*. I remarked that I had had a good time, all the women being utterly frustrated because all the men were pooves, but I suspected that, if one *were* a poove, it would be heaven on earth, and he said, Yes, he himself was a poove, and it was. Insufferable smug grin planted all over his face. Went all quiet, reminiscing, and I thought: hmmm. But it was all no good.

What I want to know is how do women actually fancy us? I mean, leaving out the perversity, the way in which the ones you desperately want don't want you, or have to be persuaded or asked nicely or have it spun out with a lot of moaning and stuff, not to mention the blacking out and wandering off. Have you had the blacking out and wandering off? You're lying there and suddenly you start thinking it's Geneva or Tuesday or you're a Hoover salesman, and then everything goes black and you have a little dream and then you come to again and it's still going on, a bit like a Mahler symphony except at least you can tell when a Mahler has finished, except for the 2nd which *keeps* finishing; the last movement even starts off like something coming to the end, and then goes on from there. Sibelius does that, too, whereas Handel just sort of peters out a lot, a nice trick if you can pull it off, which I can't. I hate Handel. Paunchy retrospective doggy-do's, at least his harpsichord stuff. Hate it. *Hate it*. Did I mention that Tracey was back? Tracey is the Flemish double and she's been away on a job for a couple of weeks, come back with £500 tucked in her G-string and I'm going to buy her a set of wooden jacks and a soundboard painting as a present. I don't know where Sharon is. Somewhere in Crouch End, I think, which is no place for a Pascal Taskin, even a green one. God knows what she's up to; she was all nicely tuned up when I last saw her, baroque pitch and Werkmeister III, but they go off you know, let them out of your sight and it's all up a semitone, equal temperament, dampers ragged, quills floppy, strings hanging out, consorting with all sorts of rubbish, anything that comes along, Böhm flutes, flat-bow fiddles, even saw one tarting around with a saxophone the other day in one of those clubs.

I mean, how the hell do you lose a harpsichord, for God's sake? They're *big*. Bigger than women, though less trouble and, when I come to think about it, slightly more difficult to lose. I don't know. I give up. I've been looking at men the last few days – you know, *peering* – and it simply won't do. It's all bum-cleft and hairy back, armpits and Y-fronts, and the thought of being chased around a hotel room by someone in public relations is just incomparably nasty. Nothing to do with the generally lamentable standard of grooming and presentation, either. The ones who have read *GQ* are absolutely the worst. It's got a woman editor now, and how nice that that horrible man has gone, the precious one with the house which was an *absolute art form dear*, the one with the wardrobe restricted to black and white: you can either have a house which is an *absolute art form* OR a wardrobe restricted to black and white, but having both at once is a bit too much. Almost over the top.

Of course, real men don't read *GQ* because they aren't the ones who like to swot up on the semiology of the turnup. Real men have anoraks and read magazines about *things*. Inanimate things. Aeroplanes. Cars. Guns. Sportsmen. Businessmen. Money.

I saw two of them in the pub the other day. Well . . . I *eyed* them. You know, practising to be a homosexual. It didn't work. They were in public relations, forty-ish, one with a northern accent and a smashed head like some monstrous pubis, the other one florid and bogus, and they were using those wretched phrases that people like them use ('So you are in cahoots, if you will, with Norman? At the as it were *cutting edge* of his shall we say new policy?' 'Yes . . . yes . . . I'm sworn as it were to secrecy if you will but fundamentally his er *scheme* his *scheme* er is to use cardboard cameras and bits of wood with sheepskin on to look like microphones at the er if you will *events*, thus . . .' 'Yes! Yes! Thus, if I anticipate your er drift, meaning, er, the, shall we say, *client* will believe ITN is if you will *covering* the alleged *event* and we can always say, Oh the news editor must have pulled the item . . . Yes! Yes!')

No. No. You couldn't. I couldn't. The actual, the, er, if you will, the loathsome *bottom stuff* would be perhaps possible, but you'd have to listen to their conversation and they'd want to be impressing you all the time and telling you stuff, and what I want to know is: *how do you do it*? I mean, those of you who are women. How? Can you shut the buggers up? Do they ever stop? Do they ever catch sight of themselves and *laugh*? God knows, I can imagine most things – I can even imagine that Bach knew what he was doing when he wrote that awful French Overture, though Tracey will have none of it – but I can't imagine them ever just not being awful, not even for a bit. I do wish you'd tell me, then I can be a poove. Not that I'm looking for a relationship, you understand, not a *relationship*, I'm not ready for that, there's too much to sort out. I have to find out, you know, what I really want. I'd just like to as it were if you will shall we say . . . *understand*.

7

HELLO; IT'S ME. I've had the, the, anyway, I told him where to get off, I said 'Put that back,' you should have seen him! Red as a, what is it?

No; really? You wouldn't have thought it of her, not if you met her mother, as common as you please.

Came off the boat with a set of Vuitton luggage and a face like a used teabag. Of course they were never the same since the dog died.

He could never stomach wallflowers. Used to go mad, Rawlplugs all over the place and no room for the doings.

Hang on, there's the, the, who is he?, down the road, number 46, the one with that jacket. I'd better let him into the cellar or there'll be, there'll be, you know, and it's a bugger, that is.

It's worse since those Pakis took over, Egyptians, what are they? Forty-one pee and that's just the small one, they never work properly, halfway through and all you get is a dribble.

Harold was like that, finicky about his clothes, you couldn't get him out of the car sometimes; he'd sit there saying 'Just a mo,' but it never was, that's the funny thing.

Who was the other one? You know: the other one, came from, where was it, you know the one I mean, he was going to grow a moustache once but never did.

Like one of those little shirts with an earwig on, they used to wear them for the tennis.

Yes. I don't hold with darts myself. Too much of it. I mean, I've got nothing against it but thingy, thingy never liked it, didn't hold with it, he was against all that sort of stuff.

I wouldn't go in anywhere with a yellow sign over it, not for food. Yellow's wrong for food.

She left him in the end, after he gave her a pink cashmere twinset for Christmas. Threw it straight back at him and out of the door, that was the end, over with a capital eff. Well after that he always kept it by him, the twinset, handy like, you never knew when you might want to get rid of someone like that.

She was the one who . . .

God knows it didn't put you-know-who off in the end but it's my guess he'd been practising, he came back from Droitwich with a forearm like Rod Laver and his eye out, and never mind the new Rolex ticking away, not a word about that, cool as you please, how would it be if everyone did?

And only twenty-three. It was the week away with that bone man did it.

Got to be the centre of attention, that's his problem, flouncing out of the room so that people will talk about him behind his back, never happier than when he's up a ladder but that was before the business with the manhole: who'd of thought it? There was nothing wrong with the old Cortina that money couldn't buy but the other one was as queer as a nine-bob note.

Green's worse.

So it all had to come out, there and then, not even time for a Bovril sandwich, she was, like, haemorrhaging, it was, you know, like haemorrhaging, like haemorrhaging.

I done them for four hours in warm water and they come out all yellowish, all them outer leaves, they used to take them off but not any more, oh no, you're paying for them, it's all weight, that is.

He used to collect them but that was before his artificial leg, you could have got an umbrella in them days if you knew who to have a word with. Nowadays it's all forms. Have you tried to get a vase, just an ordinary one, nothing fancy? I don't bother, don't make me laugh, I said, don't bloody make me laugh, stick 'em in the back room along with rest, if it's good enough for Victor Sylvester it's good enough for me. I told her. Juan-les-Pins? Don't give me that. Bollocks to Juan-les-Pins. Bollocks to it. Bollocks.

There was ashes everywhere. The vicar wasn't half embarrassed, didn't know where to put himself. Never laid eyes on him before and there in the middle of everything was this tooth, large as life. They don't burn. When you go you have to give your pacemaker back, but not our Karen, oh no. So it comes up to us, sniffing around, and she says 'Oooh, look at the knackers on that, our Deirdre! I wonder what sex it is?' It was the same one as had that bubble-car, he was awful, he was, own business or no own business, I says to him 'They'll feel your collar in the end, my lad,' and was I right? The bogies may be thick but they aren't stupid. Whoever heard of a gynaecologist with a DA?

Boy-mad, morning noon and night, she was, but then she got asphyxiated and it put her right off. Woolworths is no place for those sort of goings-on. I told him, I said, 'Put that paper down, this is a launderette, not a bleeding library.' Well! But you never see a nig-nog in a Rolls-Royce, it would look all wrong and they know it. BMWs . . . now you're talking.

Standing there with his thing hanging out, I said, 'Who do you bleeding think you are? Doctor bleeding Johnson?' So he knocks off a tenner and I took it home there and then and it's never been the same since. There was a grinding noise and Wayne says, 'Blimey, Mam, there's grit in the pleats.' I says, 'You watch your lip, you little basket, or I'll knock your block off.' And off she goes, meek as you please, and next thing you know they've unscrewed it at the mains, right outside, standing there in the street, never even rang the bleeding bell.

He traded it in for another one. I couldn't tell the difference but they weren't the same. One of them had an accent but I don't know which. Didn't matter to Len, though; rain or shine, once he was up his shed, that's that, hours could go by for all he cared, it could get dark, anything. Once it come on to rain, no warning, nothing. So I says to myself, Right, he can bloody well stay there, I'm not bleeding wasting gas on a whole bunch of carol-singers. So he turns round and says, 'Thirty-three pee,' and not a smile on his face.

How many of them?

No he never.

Ta-ra, then.

26

8

OTEMPORA; O MORES! O sancta simplicitas! O felix culpa! O nameless evil in the form of a shapeless blob! Take your pick, as I have taken mine, but my advice is; go for the blob.

It was one of those happy coincidences. Woman A rang me earlier in the week and I said 'Hello, how are you?' and she burst into tears and I said, 'Funnily enough, so am I,' and told her my troubles for a bit because people like to hear these things. Accuracy is important but compromise is essential: pause for the right word, as I did (it turned out to be 'evanescent' but by then it was too late) and next thing you know, woman A has hijacked the conversation, snarling, 'To hell with that, what about me. I am being pursued by a nameless evil in the form of a shapeless blob.'

Well . . . we Bargepoles know what to do when someone tells you she is being pursued by an n.e. in the f. of an s.b: you walk them through the relevant pages of the *Rituale Romanum*, murmur a few comforting words to the effect that there'll be another one along in a minute, plenty of fish on the beach and it's always darkest before it gets darker still, then you put the telephone down, cackle maniacally and sacrifice a goat.

I learned long ago to keep a goat by me at all times, a trick I picked up from this guy – just a typical Iraqi revolutionary moonlighting as janitor-cum-*ceremoniarius* at an Amsterdam latex-and-dildo club – and which has come in handy on all those occasions when one suddenly is overwhelmed by the need to commit an atrocity. There's so little inconvenience with goats: no need to trump up the evidence, hold the show trial, shout, boast or indulge in flaky self-justification: just grasp your goat firmly and commit the atrocity of your choice. I recommend it.

Of course, all these things are conducted under the secrecy of the confessional, so when woman B came round for a bit of a chat I said: 'Guess what? Woman A is being pursued by a nameless evil in the form of a shapeless blob,' and woman B said 'Oh – does she mean you?'

At first I was hurt. I see myself as a poet, a pilot, a lover, a musician of genius, and sometimes as Judy Garland in *A Star is Born* – dear, brave Judy, how she suffered, her heart was breaking and yet she went out there, night after night, all the hungry eyes of the people consuming her, *consuming* her – but not, in general, as a nameless evil in the form of a shapeless blob.

Yet the more I thought about it, the more attractive it became. Hitherto, my life has been ruled by the principles of emotional candour, complex pharmaceuticals and financial chicanery, but look where it has got me: holed up in this goat-stained room with a comprehensive selection of liturgical sourcebooks, a duffel-bag stuffed with lurid pornography and Barbie and Ken snarling on the other side of the wall (their accents slip with rage or lubricity). I wake alone, usually to the sound of the telephone bell as ex-lovers ring me for a bit of a talk: they couldn't abide me when we were *à deux* but now I am their close chum, dear old me, such a sweet, sweet person, there are so few men you can *talk* to, really, but he's always so *kind*, so *understanding*, there are times when it really helps to talk things over. I never really realised it when we were together but he's really terribly *wise*.

O yes. I sleep alone, cuddling endearments to my pillow (I don't want to get involved with the goat, it wouldn't want a *relationship*, better to keep it light, just go on doing what we do and see what happens, a goat needs *space*, it needs *time* to grow and be itself, it has a lot of complexities in its life to come to terms with), but, by God, *I understand women*. I understand women to the point where I think I shall throw up if I ever see another one again, particularly if she looks at me in that aggressive, kittenish, you-won't-get-into-*my*-knickers-but-I'll-kill-you-if-you-don't-at-least-*try* fashion which is as subtle as a neon sign in six-foot letters saying *I am going to screw you up for being a man*.

I found myself sitting opposite Shere Hite the other day, all ego, voice and hairdo. For a moment I wanted to say 'I read all your books and now I know what women want' and then whip her skirt over her head shouting 'Centaurs! All the fiends! There's hell, there's darkness, there is the sulphurous pit, burning, scalding, stench, consumption: fie, fie, fie! pah, pah!' but I realised that I simply don't know how to pronounce 'Pah!' – it's one of those words like 'Imph'm' or 'Pshaw' or 'Tut!' that can get you into more trouble than all those smart-arse polysyllables – so I asked the barman for an ounce of civet (straight up, no twist, no cherry, no umbrella), sweetened my imagination and pushed along.

Much better to be a nameless evil in the form of a shapeless blob. I shall make people unhappy: I know where I am going to start. I am going to start with woman C. I will do such things as will rock her on her Manolo Blahnik heels. Within the week she will be barking mad and believe herself to be a tree. I shall also deal with woman D, who is nothing to do with me but the *inamorata* of my poor friend Weeb, who sees himself as a Howard Hawks character but has in reality made of himself the most notorious geck and gull that e'er invention played on. Egged on by me, he has been taking white roses to a sweet-mouthed Soho bed-show shill, fired by fantasies of courtly love and sweetest consummation that transcends all rank. His dark lady of the doorways shows signs of softening and if I do not act fast the poor grizzled *Rosenkavalier* runs a serious risk of succeeding and being happy and, what is worse, making woman D happy too. So I shall be round there myself, clutching a stick of broccoli, accompanied by two huge boogies to hold her down.

Nameless evil in the form of a shapeless blob? O yes. Watch your step. That's me there, at your shoulder. I'm the thing in the airing cupboard, the funny smell in your briefcase, the squeak in your shoe: when you wander around foreign towns in the small hours, it's me you're looking for. Will you find me? O no need: I've already found *you*.

30

9

THE BABY WAS the worst thing. Gosh it was horrid, like a turnip-ghost or a reject, all shiny and goggling with one of those damned faces. You could see it in 30 years' time, a booming meaty dud with a huge shirt and too many credit cards. They are the worst, but its parents were the worst, too, toting it around the party, bringing a special rug for it to play on, giving it things it didn't like in the presence of people who didn't like it and wished it wasn't there.

I don't mind babies, on the whole, but this one was an accessory. You could see that its parents thought they were being terribly smart, instinctively forming disagreeable little *tableaux* representative of the current and vegetative *Zeitgeist*. They crooned to it, smiled at it, tickled it, put it on its rug, all the time quite clearly thinking that *we* were all *noticing*, all thinking 'Oh look! They are crooning, how sweet, they are smiling at it, how sweet, they are tickling it, how sweet.'

Five out of ten. We *were* all noticing . . . and we *were* all thinking: 'Ugh, they are crooning, they are smiling at it, they are tickling it, best thing to do would be to rape the mother, disembowel the father and then rustle up a skewer and a campfire, babies make great kebabs, or so I am told.'

It wasn't very Nineties stuff to think, I'll admit, but one isn't a very Nineties person. This cocooning is grim. I bought a special jersey to cocoon in, 16-ply cream cashmere, and I hate it. Usually if you get the clothes right the rest will follow but I tried it the other day and it was disastrous. Perhaps I should have been wearing the horrid shoes as well. Perhaps I should have gone down to Yohji Yamamoto and bought one of those expressions cocooners wear which look as though someone has just clapped a handful of cold rice pudding around where their balls would have been if it were still the Eighties.

Whatever, it was all a mistake. I put on the jersey, arranged my features into something which a partially-socialised Malagasy forest-dweller with a visual handicap might have mistaken for marginally incipient benignancy, and got into the big chair with the popsy. We snuggled up as specified in the operating manual, and discussed matters of concern to Nineties people: the environment, pair-bonding, finding our souls after the hurly-burly of rampant materialism, but then I came unstuck on the trees. I *hate* the stuff about trees, how we should save the rain forest because of all the things the plants contain which could provide Miracle Cures. Nonsense. We have quite enough Miracle Cures anyway. It's getting increasing hard to find anything to die of, and when something *does* turn up, like Aids or drunken driving, we make the most abominable fuss, as if God is being unfair and arbitrary and picking on us. Of *course* He is being unfair and arbitrary and picking on us: that's what He's for, and a good thing too. Much better to be created by a complete bastard like this one than by the sort of God who wears puffy shoes, is really into cereal, and won't go anywhere without His wife.

The reason for not chopping down the rain forest is nothing to do with Miracle Cures or ozone layers or anything else. It's just that they aren't ours, and we should leave them alone. As for this poop about the planet being at risk, it's nonsense. What is at risk is us. The planet doesn't give a hang. Does anyone really believe that one day some benighted Brazilian will bulldoze one tree too many and the earth will say, 'Right, that's it, *that's bloody IT*,' and implode? Of course not. All that'll happen is that we will choke to death and a good thing too, then something else can have a go, and never mind if it's ugly or got a shell or too many eyes: as long as it doesn't invent tourism, broadcasting, the anorak, fast food and politics I will be on its side even if I'm extinct.

None of these animadversions went down particularly well in the cocooning scenario, and before long I got angry and tried to give her one, swearing furiously out of the side of my mouth and scrabbling at her clothes. And *that* didn't go down too well either so I had to send her off in a dudgeon which, fortunately, was ticking over outside the door. I thought of phoning up for another one and trying again, omitting the tree stuff and going straight for the giving-her-one stuff, but then I thought, no, sod it. I might as well die out on my own and anyway the nasty one, the one I really love, was nowhere around, see if I care.

Perhaps one should practise a bit first. When I was fifteen I used to practise kissing on the pillow. It's almost as good as the real thing except that women aren't full of feathers – would that they were – and many of my happiest hours have been spent whispering honeyed endearments into a 20-ounce bag of goose down, plus, unlike a woman you can plump them up when they go flat on you. But the new books don't like surrogates. 'Learn to love yourself,' they say, which seems silly to me. It's not like the behind-the-bike-shed stuff at school. That's straightforward and only takes a couple of minutes, but this takes hours. Hair on the palms of the hands, going mad, going blind, all that is small beer compared with having to sit on one's interminable own in an armchair, with one arm around one's own shoulder, stroking one's hair with the other hand, and murmuring into one's own ear a lot of tripe about security, loyalty and non-penetrative sex, all of which is a foregone conclusion anyway.

And can you imagine the pornography? Pictures of people asleep on their own side of the bed. Stories about babies. Glamourwear catalogues full of jerseys. Suburban parties where everyone throws their car-keys into a hat and walks home to save the environment. It is going to be horrible. The Comfy Chair has become grim reality: so comfy that we'll never be able to get out of it, and we'll all starve to death.

THERE I WAS, with two agony aunts all to myself. Went for a drink with one, and we were sitting peaceably enough discussing barnacles, as one does, when another one came over. 'I'm an agony aunt, too!' she cried; 'I just had to come and introduce myself!' So there I was: two agony aunts, and I couldn't think of any agony. *Esprit d'escalier* is a monstrous affliction. I don't have to tell you that as my taxi lurched home my heart, too, lurched within the mass–produced Swiss roll I use instead of a body, and unburdened itself of all sorts of fascinatingly, coruscatingly dreadful things which it had been keeping to itself all evening.

There aren't any agony aunts for men. Or agony uncles. Why is that? I suppose it's because we are big and strong and don't have problems like a pack of cissy women. Or if we do, we have learnt how to deal with them. What you do is bottle them up and then one day someone refuses to go to bed with you any more, or indeed at all, or in the first place, or not yet because things are a bit difficult and she can't face complicating her life, or it's the wrong time of the month, or the wrong time of the year, or any of the other excuses they have available to them, the bastards, whereas if *we* do that we are offensive, impotent, spineless or queer.

At that point, being Big and Strong, we don't fanny around with agony aunts or agony uncles, oh no. We just go barking mad and end up in a converted country house bouncing off the latex anaglypta, howling at the moon and drumming frantically with our rubber cutlery.

Is this the best way to go about things? Yes, it probably is. It puts fear into the hearts of those who reject us and gives us the chance to have a good shout and a cry, things which are normally denied to us by the quotidian necessity of wearing suits, driving big cars, and calling people Mr

Wilmshurst ('About the interim figures, Mr Wilmshurst . . .'), and, indeed, the necessity of earning all that money to impress the women who will not be impressed by it at all and who will consequently drive us barking mad. It all fits together so neatly that, well, one can't help detecting the hand of what's-his-name there, or am I wrong? Thingy. God. Never mind trees, birds and sunsets, the Divine afflatus is most perceptible in the elegant intricacy of human misery, that's what I always say, and I shall be saying it a lot from now on.

I have decided to become an agony uncle, you see, for men. Women writing in will get short shrift, or indeed, as I become more cynical, no shrift at all. The agony aunts told me that 99% of their letters are about Why Won't My Man Make A Commitment, so we can deal with that right now: the reason he won't make a commitment is because you have made it quite clear from your behaviour that you would either reject him or, if not, make his life a misery. He has become as wary as a trench-bound swaddy; the passions, which you interpret as gurgling and lovely, are to him the sound of shrapnel passing overhead. Who has to ask first? Who has to keep ringing up? Who has to go on and on and on in a state of uncertainty which would *kill* you, my honeys? Who has to make the pass? Who has to still his beating heart and call people Mr Wilmshurst?

So that's *that* one dealt with. Nor do I want to hear about periods (I have suffered premenstrual tension for 20 years now and am still waiting) or feelings of physical unworthiness (I have short legs and *no tits at all* but one thing I do know is that anyone who predicates her emotional happiness on the physical or aesthetic response of some horrid, hairy-pawed, sclerotic-fisted tabloid reader with a beer gut and the emotional subtlety of a late Victorian lavatory is asking for everything she gets).

This will be for men.

It could get boring. The agony aunts told me that men occasionally write in and it's always about the size of their willies. Most of them think their willies are too small, but some, in tones of furtive boasting, complain that they are too big. I personally have had no trouble with mine, although it has caused problems for others, more of the *Oh for God's sake go to sleep* or *I'm sorry, I just don't feel that way about you* kind rather than the commando-style heavy-injury offensive operations which one feels would be more appropriate on occasions.

So . . . no willy letters will be answered, either. Just remember, chaps, whatever they tell you, size *does* count, and if you're inadequate, you're inadequate, and you might as well give up. But what a silly little appendage to worry about anyway. God could have done much better: if He wanted to suspend something from our pubic symphysis, a Swiss army knife would be infinitely more useful, or how about a saxophone? Look on the bright side, that's the thing.

I can't really deal with your emotional problems either, because I have little sympathy with your naïvety. You can't tell whether she's interested? That's because a woman who is interested will make herself unavailable, fail to return your telephone calls, be cool and noncommittal; whereas a woman who is not interested at all will do exactly the same things. It's called 'playing hard to get'; their mothers teach it to them; the only thing you can do is wait until she crushes your balls, which she will surely do, one way or the other; harsh and instant rejection is the least time-consuming, but you may have to marry her and stick around for years until, eventually, the knee comes hurtling upwards in an immaculate Flying Arkwright.

As for sex . . . straightforward, I'm afraid. If you aren't having a fulfilling sex life and your woman seems to have gone off you, there is nothing you can do. She doesn't fancy you. Anything else? Well . . . if there is, just pull yourselves together and be a man. I've gone off the whole idea, so don't bother writing.

II

MANY OF YOU have written in to say 'It's all very well you banging on about these skinny women with big hooters, but what do I do when I'm irritated by someone in a restaurant?'

Fair enough. I have two things to say. One is, from now on it's small brunettes for me, and the other is, look no further. Etiquette is a tough business but I am here to help. Number One in a series, personally researched by me this very evening in Kettner's, the excitingly fashionable Soho nite-spot, where the cream of Hendon's conveyancing solicitors mingle willy-nilly with people who are quite happy at Marks and Spencers because, say what you like, the career structure is well mapped out. And their girlfriends, too, choicest toothsome morsels of the 34A toxic shock society. Yeah? Yeah. Lights. Camera. Action.

LOCATION: Soho. Big room. Champagne the other end, overpriced. Food this end, hamburgers and pizzas, extra everything please, underpriced, so that you say 'Oh look at the bill, how cheap it is, we must come here more often,' because you have forgotten how much you spent on champagne at the other end, earlier. Pianist who looks as though he would have a wig if he wasn't the sort of person who was afraid of other people saying 'Oh look at the pianist, he's got a wig or am I wrong?' They are; but they wouldn't be.

TIME: Weekday evening.

CAST: Innumerable men in suits trying to look as though they aren't men in suits. Strange feeling that some of the men in suits have only just put their suits on, specially, so that they can say to their women 'Just come from work, hell of a day, been in a meeting, David is being an absolute pain in the arse about the press release and what with the trade show on Saturday, well, you know, well, and how was, another glass of, er, Bollinger, how can they charge £26.85 for Bollinger?, another, er?, anyway, how was er your day akshly?'

MORAL DILEMMA: These are awful people. *Awful*. They stare at each other, hungry, salivating, emanating evil, the charm of a stale Aertex blouse in a locker room. The women are old enough to be one's father and should be minced. The men have BMWs. Some of the men even have BMW convertibles. What they would really like is an over-achieving woman with an eccentric wardrobe and A Mind Of Her Own, but what they actually have are amanuenses with sequential visual recall difficulties. Obviously one should hate these men. Obviously one should murmur rude things to them as one leaves, causing them to cry. Their womenfolk will despise them and there will be no cocooning for them, not now, not ever.

But does one do this? No. Surrounded by a parade of suited grotesques, one bides one's time, which is rapidly running out. A man comes in. He is fat. He has a goatee beard. He is accompanied by a woman and a plastic carrier bag. He ignores the former and gropes around in the latter. He is morally unacceptable. He is preposterous, a parody of himself, wearing monstrous clothes, a foolish grey jersey, a *horrid* jersey, a *minicab-driver*'s jersey if we are to be precise. He is an American. He grunts. From the bag he produces a pipe. He unscrews it. There is a horrible smell. He cleans it, clucking and drooling repellently. The woman does a crossword puzzle. He produces another pipe. He unscrews it. There is a horrible smell. He cleans it. The woman continues with the crossword puzzle. He produces another pipe. Then another. Then another. Six in all.

Then he roots around in his plastic bag again. His hands are filthy. His belly wobbles. His eyes pop. If there is a God, he will have a stroke, but there isn't and he doesn't, producing instead six felt Pipe Bags, anally retentive pouches for his little friends, from his plastic bag. Into the Pipe Bags go the pipes, one by one. Out they come again, as he realises that some are in the wrong Bags. In they go, into the right Pipe Bags. Out they come again, to be filled with cheap yellow tobacco from a nasty bakelite BaccyFlap. Two sit on the table beside him, reeking. He snarls at the woman. He waggles a fat finger at the waiter: spit, juice and tar fly around. 'Gimme nother ashtray,' he growls. 'Gimme nother serviette.'

CORRECT FORM: What does one do about this? You may think one gives a subtle pained glance to one's companion, indicating contempt for the joke 'man' and sympathy for his poor companion. You would be wrong. Although it is un-Nineties to make a fuss, this man has said 'serviette', and must be punished. Correct behaviour is therefore to adopt an Argentinian accent, present his woman with a flower, stroke his neck, and accuse him of churlishness and impotence in an undertone. He will then go apeshit and lurch from his chair, shouting. At this point, the master of correct form giggles winsomely and tells him he is a big boy who probably has no trouble in getting girlfriends. This should be done in a Paisley accent. The joke 'man' will then get very confused trying to work out whether it was a Paisley accent the first time you addressed him. Correct form is now to skip out of the 'restaurant'. Your opponent will follow you, shouting abuse. Once a crowd has gathered, you run away with the prettiest available woman (if in doubt, bring one with you) and have wild sex until dawn. Your opponent will not have any such thing (which is why he has to take six pipes to a restaurant) but he will acquire a thick coating of cholesterol around his coronary arteries. Ideally, you should go back the following day and do it again, and the next day, and the next, until he lurches from his chair and dies of a heart attack. At this point, you will have become a Master of Etiquette, and can apply for the job as Ambassador to Iraq.

I HAVE HERE (*coughs, wheezes, rummages through blitzed desk with palsied frenzy*) a photograph . . . of . . . myself. It is vile, minatory, pornographic. If you had a pornograph, you could see for yourself.

I was on a boat with some people. A *bateau-mouche*, one of those things which crawl up and down the Seine at night, with banks of floodlights on each side to illuminate the waterfront. Thirty-seven million tourists get on and are filled up with lobster and wine while a lascivious woman plays the harp. One boards the vessel in a state of cringing and shifty self-excoriation, looking forward to a horrible time. There are Japanese by the trunk-load: the men look bitter while the women walk as though, immediately prior to setting out, they have been subjected to multiple indignities. There are vegetable Scandinavians, and Americans trying very hard to pretend they aren't, although they haven't quite decided what they're pretending they *are*. There is, invariably, a party of Belgians in dinner jackets, one of whom is an imbecile. Then there are more Japanese, just like the first lot of Japanese. Funny thing about the Japanese: they really don't know why everyone else hates them, although everyone else knows why with absolute clarity.

And then there are the businessmen. Lots of businessmen, entertaining other businessmen or, in my case, journalists. Most of the businessmen look upon the occasion as a dreadful ordeal, like presentations. Businessmen *hate* presentations. One businessman stands up in a darkened room and shows 'overheads' and says a whole lot of things which are untrue. The other businessmen sit in the darkened room, maddened with sensory deprivation, loathing the businessman who is talking to them. Then they repeat the performance, changing places. This is called 'communication' and is said to be what business is 'all about'. It is clearly nonsense. All it requires is that one brave businessman breaks the chain and it would all be all right.

Think of the other things which could be stopped if the chain were broken. Doing-it-yourself, for example. Wearing anoraks. Accountancy. Car-cleaning. All sorts of things. Here is a scheme for you: every householder in the country sends me a hundred quid. You wouldn't miss it, and I'd have five billion pounds which I would use to buy houses. I would then sell those houses for five thousand quid each. The bottom would *really* fall out of the housing market and we could start again at sensible pricing levels. See how easy it is when you use your brain?

Then we could stop photographs, too. Photographs are responsible for a lot of human misery. The Japanese sat down and the Swedes and imbeciles sat down and we all sat down and they gave us lobster and the boat puttered up and down the Seine. The harpist played and lovers kissed on the banks, doubtless obliged to do so in return for a retainer paid by Bateaux-Mouches de Paris SA, but never mind, and one ineluctably mellowed. One was helpless, replete with reasonable things which steadily obliterated one's initial aesthetic revulsion. The businessmen were not so bad after all. One was facing the stern and could not see the Japanese.

One found oneself resolving to be good, to live a purer life. One would get the hell out of England, with its road works and filth and ugly, ugly citizens and honking, small-minded government, its repugnant, company-car-driving premature ejaculators and fat, fat, reeking pinhead plebs, one would abandon for ever snooker and darts, Adidas, Tie Rack, ketchup, the Woolwich, joky Telecom advertisements, navel-fluff pubs and public service films telling us not to swim with our mouths full.

Why should one tolerate this? Is one not a man of dignity? Can one continue to live in a country fit only for pigs and the dispossessed? And so on. You know the feeling, perhaps:

one's *amour-propre* swells, one feels expansive, at ease in the world, benign.

And then some grinning lipless squit with a Noctilux and a flashgun comes along and takes a photograph. He has a darkroom on the boat and, just when one is feeling most expansive, he brings the photograph back. One's host orders one a print. It is terrifying. It reveals a drunk, surrounded by other drunks. The other drunks are much better looking for a start, apart from the drunk who has been placed at the next table, a prophetic *Doppelgänger*, advanced merely by five years, five gins, five stone and five chins. One's future is thereby revealed, but one's present is bad enough: this is the face and figure of one who collects bus-tickets, a small saver who buys a copulation once each quarter day and has a bathroom cabinet full of undignified remedies. We are plunged into a subculture of feeble and unconvincing passes which go unnoticed, of tiny humiliations, unsent love-letters, underwear worn two days running because it *really doesn't matter*, the rented room, green milk, tinfoil takeaway trays, chewed biros and evening newspapers.

And all from a photograph. We obsessively document our lives with 'candid' pictures and the result is misery. The blasted things *do* eat our souls and I am having no more of it. And don't tell me that the camera *does* lie. It doesn't help. So do lots of other things ('Of *course* I love you. Of *course* I'm not sleeping with anyone else') and they don't help either. Next time you see a dork behind a viewfinder, punch him in the face and rip his film out. This is the first step in the civilisation of the West. Step two? Send me the hundred quid mentioned earlier. We'll sort this all out, never fear. Would I lie to you? Of course not. Of *course* you don't look like that really. Of *course* I'm not sleeping with anyone else.

13

THE NOVELIST RANG me up this afternoon from his house in Provence to say that he had a problem. Last time he had a problem in Provence I had to perform a mercy dash to the airport, subsequently spending the entire summer sympathising with him and ending up with a bloodstream like the back room of Boot's the Chemist, so I hardened my heart. Apart from anything else, I have a nasty Ghost Train wound on my left arm, as well as other bites, scratches, bruises and throttle-marks acquired in varying circumstances and under many different degrees of provocation and culpability. The worst one is on my neck. A man flew at me in one of those pimp buildings that pimp businessmen put up to show the world what pimps they are. He accused me of sleeping with his girlfriend, and out flew the hands, whop! whop! around the neck, the thumb pressure starts and everything goes even blacker than it was already, what with the terribly dead *linguine alle vongole* and the drinking accident shortly after dawn.

I may not have to tell you people *never* to eat pasta in the bath whether or not there is big dog floating about in the water, but I did have to tell this man that I was not sleeping with his rat-like girlfriend. After a bit he believed me, but he still wasn't happy. 'Well she's certainly not sleeping with *me*, either,' he whimpered. 'Who is she sleeping with?' God how pathetic. I thought about ripping his lips off but instead I told him I knew precisely who she was sleeping with and pulled out a name at random, at which point he tried to kill me all over again.

There's a time to apply one's black-belt karate, and this is not it. Instead (and here's a tip for you, next time some bawling hack has his hands round your windpipe and the world is receding to a dot) I followed standard SAS procedure and moved towards my attacker. This destabilises them, you see. Then what you do is croak 'But it's *you* I want, really', and put your tongue down his throat. He cries 'Ugh! Ugh! O God!' and relinquishes his grip, and you run wheezing away. It's horrid, but not half as bad as being an empty on the doorstep of life.

Though I don't know, come to think of it. My friend Ralph once had to design a show which, inexplicably, featured a lot of dwarves. I suppose they thought it would be a Unique Selling Point, which probably means there was some highly paid marketing person on a retainer at the conceptualisation stage. Clenched and sickly people with that depressing sort of middle-of-the litter feeling about them. One imagines that they are rude to their wives, send their cars to be valeted, would like to dance the Lambada at Tramp and always remember to take a dirty sock with them. Or it might have been a musical version of *Snow White*.

Whatever, it had dwarves, real ones, and was a rather tense production. Eventually, the day before the dress rehearsal, one of the dwarves could stand it no longer. Stamping his foot, he swished offstage. Just as he was about to disappear into the wings, he paused, shook his fist, and, face contorted with purest *Weltschmerz*, bellowed:

'I've had it up to *here* with this midget lark.'

Absolutely right. This midget lark is not the thing, not at all, humiliation piling upon failure and defeat, and when you just want to retire to an island and fade away, horrid things happen. Like the man who rang up and said that he and his wife had been playing some dismal Fulham Road sort of game in which you have to decide which of a given pair of people you would rather go to bed with, and I had been eliminated in favour of Marcus Berkmann, official Young Person of the *Daily Mail*, which I am no longer allowed to write for on grounds which are none of your business or anyone else's. I don't particularly mind, since its editorial policy has recently drifted from the merely fascist to the barking mad, as though it is suffering from a collective astrocytoma. When they shave its head and open it like a boiled

44

egg it will be like a Hieronymous Bosch, seething. The advertising people have already spotted it, and are now promoting it on the sole remaining grounds that the ink doesn't come off on your hands. But that's not the point: the point is that if someone is poorly enough to want to go to bed with Berkmann instead of me I wish I had been informed earlier, then I could have brought him along in a little hold-all to show my murderer. Indeed, I could have stuffed the murderer into the hold-all too, and zipped it up, and left it in the pimp lobby, bulging and roiling, until the security guards blew it up, then rushed round to Fulham with a bottle of Bollinger and my trusty Leica, shouting, 'Berkmann's dead! Ha ha! Get your gear off!'

But it was too late, and thus the culmination of one of those weeks, one of the bad ones, just like all the others. The pretty agony aunt sat on my knee but then my leg went to sleep and I tripped up the stairs, barking my shin (and butting a total stranger in the balls, some small consolation). I was accused of (a) satyriasis and (b) impotence by the same woman on the same day. I poked myself in the eye with my telephone, swallowed a cufflink, and was thrown out of a nasty nightclub by a Greek who said I was eating a fish in a threatening way (threatening to whom? The fish?). The beautiful air hostess has fallen wildly in love with a man who is Something In Oil (a sardine?) and when I told the woman I love that it was all over between us she said, 'What is?' And seeking solace, I got jammed in the Ghost Train.

So when the damned novelist rang up and said he had a problem, because he had spent £600 filling his swimming-pool and now he couldn't go in because if he did he would think *This swim has cost me £600*, but if he didn't, he wouldn't, I thought, enough. No more sympathy. From now on I shall be enigmatic, taciturn, satanically moody: one of those strong silent types you read about. I didn't hesitate. I said: '   .'

It's easy when you know how.

14

THESE ARE STRANGE and savage days. The moon is full, and the quaking fruitbag who does the horoscope says I must remember the good times because the worst is over . . . well, yes; for the first time in three years I am not in love with anyone at all, and can turn my mind to the grim and twisted bleakness of reality.

We live in a sort of hog heaven. The spare rib jammed in my garburator is coming back to life by some cabalistic principle of parthenogenesis. I can hear it creaking and swelling in the U-bend as it gropes towards the daylight. Caustic soda, battery acid and boiling oxgall have all failed to stop it. Some submerged chemical memory suggested that amyl nitrate might do the trick. They sell it in my local pub, where the fruits go for safe sex and nightmarishly dangerous drinking, so I bought a whole caseload . . . but the filthy stuff came bubbling back up the plughole and within moments I was lying on the floor, stupefied with hog-stench and apocalyptic visions.

It's a good moment for visions. St John would be at home now, out on the streets somewhere, cranking it up at a fine, psychotic rate, declaiming from a makeshift podium of Radion cartons while his audience of epsilon semi-morons in Kingfisher booties scratched their shrivelled balls and tried to think of something to think about. He wouldn't last long, though; the first hint of any beast with more than the average number of heads and he would be arrested on a public order charge, trampled by police horses, and thrown into pokey for evading the poll tax.

In which there would be some irony. The poll tax is the very same hallucinogen which inspires revelations in those of us who see retribution just around the corner, hurtling towards us, running without lights, steam hissing and scraps of flesh caught in its wheels. What vicious, deviant outcast could have foreseen that the noble desire to crush the twitching woodlice of local government would be the very thing that would give Heseltine his big chance? It's impossible to conceive that even the most reptilian political heavy-hitter, splashing around in the chilly, reeking swamps of Westminster, could have said: 'Let's set it in motion! We can rely on Mikey-baby to leap on the bandwagon!'

Or is it?

No. And it doesn't matter anyway. The truth is that the monster is out. After months – years – of skulking around on the borderlines, snuffling for scraps like a little animal, after all this time just *being there*, like a cashiered pay clerk who can't drag himself away, the . . . *thing* has sprung up from floor-level, whistling and barking, red eyes gleaming, straight on to the strangely hunched shoulders of Michael Portillo.

Should we worry about Portillo? Probably we should. A man who has had to live with such physical ugliness for so long has been forged in a furnace which most of us can't even *imagine*, and that, coupled with the bitter feral desire for conquest, means that we should probably kill him with bazookas, Glaser Safety Slugs, pangas and 900-pound o-daiko drums carved from a single tree-trunk, and leave him for three days, and feed him to Komodo dragons . . . or, better still, hire the Kodo drummers to play outlandish rhythms on the bugger until he disintegrates. But that can wait. At the moment he is skittering around, claws clacking, not realising that the *gravitas* he feels is Mikey-baby's ponderous deadweight clinging to his back.

The grim truth is that Mikey-baby could well be the next Prime Minister. His yelps of 'Let's calm down a bit!' on the *Today* programme fooled nobody. Mikey-baby is in there and punching, and the cowed, drooling back-benchers are loving it . . . and if the electorate wouldn't sack the Tories in the local government elections, they certainly aren't going to throw them into the Bosphorus when the real thing comes along.

At the next General Election, Britain is going to hit bottom, and the only sound the world will hear from us thereafter is the scrabbling of our fingernails as we scrape the barrel. The contest will be between a South Wales accent and a hairdo, and the hairdo will win, and we will become a Berni Inn for the rest of Europe, with drab, styleless dishes served in a mocked-up 'theme' setting to puffed-up businessmen . . .

So that is that. We are finished. The Thatcher revolution has brought inflation, rioting, public squalor, private cynicism, massive debt and the near-destruction of our culture by a pack of round-shouldered accountants in grubby trousers. Our infrastructure is crumbling, our food stinks, and nobody has done a damn thing about the weather.

Why am I worrying about this? Because it's my birthday today. Because, as I said, I'm not in love with anyone any more and so at last I can go away, preferably to some country where the only women are covered in matted hair and threadwarts. Because I may *have* to go away, very soon. Because the idea of a powerful and unified Europe is at last becoming a reality, despite AIDS and acid rain and Margaret Thatcher . . . and because we aren't going to be part of it. There's a couple of things left to do. I have to get the spare rib out of the garburator. I need to find my Banana Republic bush hat. There's a woman I need to sleep with in order to close a particularly warped and atavistic episode. And by the time that's all sorted out, the Channel Tunnel will be open, but I'm not going down it: it won't take them long to realise what's coming their way, and they'll just open the sluices and drown the whole pack of us like rats in a drain.

15

IWAS THINKING about something else. What? Can't remember. The moment I realised I was thinking about something else, I started thinking about that, you see, and lost track of the something else. Whatever it was.

No loss, really. It could have been anything, and what an opportunity for self-congratulation: perhaps I was thinking about lattice theory, Venetian tablature, the rain forests: a giant intellect could be throbbing away beneath my greying temples, and even if I am unaware of it, its prestige is not impaired.

It's curious, though, the intellect gradually going underground, faculties devolving themselves into the subconscious mind without consent or consultation. I found myself in the lavatory the other day without the slightest idea what I was doing there. Simple observation solved *that* problem, but how many others are there which escape my notice? How many times have I been unaware of what I was doing without even being aware that I was unaware of it? Perhaps I am a figure of fun, laughed at behind my back, *in front of* my back, even: I'd never notice, not as things are.

Does it happen to everyone? A woman started talking to me the other day in the Groucho club and I hadn't the faintest idea who she was, not even after she had explained at some length not only who she was but what she wanted from me. I wonder what she wanted.

Perhaps it is the drink, or maybe the cigarettes, or maybe it is the drugs, although I don't hold with drugs. Everyone gets terribly excited about Ecstasy but I don't hold with it myself. The point of it is to prolong and intensify sexual pleasure but I can do that quite satisfactorily on my own simply by going to sleep and as for the rest of you, I'd suggest you would be better advised to keep your clothes on. If you are honest with yourselves you will admit that the main pleasure of sex is looking forward to it. When it happens, you don't enjoy it. No: don't argue: *you don't enjoy it*. You are nervous and angry, you don't like the people you are doing it with, your mind keeps wandering and you are ashamed of your body.

We all have to confront unpleasant truths about ourselves. Honesty is the best policy. Who said that? What a nasty, twisted, evil little shit he must have been, seven identical suits, putty shoes and a mother. I have always found honesty to be absolutely the worst policy imaginable on these few occasions when, forced into an ethical corner by some barking woman with the emotional *largesse* of a cobra, I have had no option but to recite the grim facts. They always say things like 'I can handle anything if only I know the score,' but as soon as you tell them the score they go batshit and start demanding a recount or, failing that, blood.

But that's how it's going to have to be from now on, now that my mind has started to go. Successful duplicity demands razor-sharp reflexes and it's all very well telling people that you are a Hungarian gynaecologist if you remember that that's what you have told them. Lose one's grip and things fall apart, a maxim which holds as true for life as for gynaecology, as do many items of that peculiarly subliterate form of disconnected imbecility known as 'folk wisdom'. I suppose the only major difference is that with gynaecology you at least stand a chance of getting out under your own steam, a question which professional eschatologists have largely ignored, perhaps because they never thought of it but more likely because they did think of it but forgot what it was.

There will thus be a lot of changes. This truth business will profoundly alter the course of whatever it was they handed out to me instead of a life. People will know my credit rating. There will be no more hurried trips round to Uncle to pop other people's property so that I can take expensive women out to hot snail dinners. The people who believe that I am

Hungarian will have to face the fact that they are no more in possession of the facts than the small coterie of admirers whom I have tried to bring into conformity with the fact that I am black. Several people will have to confront the truth that I have no intention at all of going to bed with them, and several others will come to realise that I am determined to do precisely that and there is nothing whatever they can do about it.

There will be professional changes, too. Certain publishers will find themselves disappointed, and some will find themselves frothing with impotent rage. My accountant will realise that he has been living in a state of prelapsarian and inarticulate bliss, and I bet he starts articulating like buggery when he finds out. The thin, bald people around me, with huge Adam's apples wobbling up and down in their necks which they have the crust to use to say things like 'Good morning!' to me, will find that, instead of nodding curtly, I stand my ground and describe them to themselves, just in case I forget, do you see?

It will, I suspect, be a simple life, devoid of incident. I will be able to concentrate all my energies on trying to concentrate on what I was trying to concentrate all my energies on. You will not be able to unsettle me: secure in my cocoon of fluffy pink malignancy, I shall simply smile and nod, wondering why I am doing so. Eventually I shall float away on a cloud of mute asynchronous *aperçus*, drooling a little (perhaps) from the corner of the mouth, or perhaps from elsewhere. The world will come to mean nothing. I shall be self-contained, inviolable, almost Californian in the solipsistic intensity of my detachment. And then watch out. I shall be a television personality, and rich, and it will start all over again.

16

ON THE PRINCIPLE that being thoroughly wicked and nasty is preferable to keeping one's nose clean and paying the poll tax, I feel obliged to support the Provisional IRA, but my sympathy is being badly stretched. It's not that your men shoot people and blow them up, because that's what you do if you're a Provo. To say that one would sympathise with them if only they would be less violent is like saying one would support the Pope if only he would drop all the God stuff – a position, in fact, with which I agree, but it's my column and if you don't like it you can bugger off and write your own. You'll run out of ideas within a month and the pay is derisory, but you're not going to listen to me whatever I say so I might as well keep my gob shut.

The trouble with your men is their sheer incompetence. The average Provo atrocity could nowadays be summed up as *wham, BANG, sorry, ma'am*, and that just won't do. The Carlton Club bomb is yet another example of your men's incompetence. They are stuck in the past, believing that the Carlton Club is the very centre of the British establishment. It is nothing of the sort. That is merely newcasters' theme-park talk. The *real* establishment is all pushy grammar school people in unsuitable shoes, and the poor old boobies of St James's are just kept on for the tourists to gawp at.

I am not even sure why your men want to strike at the 'heart' of the 'establishment'. I suppose the idea is that we would all become terribly shocked and upset if they succeeded in blowing up a few politicians, and immediately exercise our franchise to demand a settlement of their demands. This is twisted and feral thinking, the consequence of eating green potatoes in all likelihood. First of all, if the daycent folk of Britain *were* outraged at the blowing-up of politicians, there would be nothing we could do about it at all. The

Government ignores our outrage until it's time for the next election, when they all start greasing up like mad. Secondly, a successful blowing-up operation would mean that there was nobody left to call an election or referendum anyway. And thirdly, nobody would be particularly outraged or upset.

That't the important point: threatening to kill politicians in order to frighten us is like someone saying to me 'If you don't leave my wife alone I will break into the Inland Revenue computer and erase your file'. Your men, I imagine, are so excited by the idea of the Great Political Struggle that they assume we are, too, instead of realising that one of the nicest things imaginable to the thinking Briton is the thought of a ruthless, efficient and comprehensive blowing-up of politicians. We're all *Sun* readers now, and nothing excites us more than a politician meeting sudden and violent retribution, as much as anything else because we don't actually believe they exist anyway: reality and image are blurred and we'd be just as chuffed if the Thatch bit the dust as we were when they shot JR.

Your men the Provos should take my advice and go for our support. That doesn't mean they have to stop letting off bombs, merely that they have to let off *sensible* bombs. They must *immediately* stop blowing up harmless people and even politicians' spouses, who already have enough on their plates with being married to politicians. And I would suggest that they leave politicians out of it altogether. Blown-up politicians only excite us briefly because, as aforesaid, we don't think they are really real nor do we much care about them. Instead, they should concentrate on blowing up significant enemies of our happiness, and we would grow to love them and want to give them their way.

If they want to blow things up on the European mainland, they could start with *The European*, or failing that, the I M Pei pyramid in the Louvre, and follow that with blowing up whoever decided to pull down the Berlin Wall, thus destroying the last bit of Europe which hasn't become a Levis-wearing, Budweiser-drinking, condom-wearing outpost of America.

While they are at it, they could blow up whichever executives of Levis, Budweiser, NatWest and Swatch are responsible for considering the idea of advertising their nasty products on huge television screens in discotheques.

The death list is endless. Marks and Spencers for buying Brooks Brothers. Anyone who says 'Hi, Richard' to Richard Jobson. Art Fry for inventing Post-It Notes. Marla Maples, for humping Donald Trump then getting asked to 'act' in *Dallas*, thus setting a lousy example to all those other women who think they can open doors by opening their legs. Whoever it is who thinks Australia is exciting, so that we not only have Fosters and Castlemaine advertisements but also the ones for that horrid microwave pot noodle stuff, and endless Australian soaps and series and the preposterous Shell advertisement, all featuring common, sweating people in Akubra hats, giving totally the wrong impression of Australia which is in fact full of decent, loyal, handsome women with good muscle tone who root like rattlesnakes and can't pass a prick.

And, of course, my stinking producer friend who after years of trouble and despair culminating in two twelve-months of unrequited love has finally found happiness in the arms of his beloved, against all odds. That makes me *really* angry, and I can hardly breathe with the amount of cocaine I have had to put up my nose to cope with my grief and rage.

The trouble is, the Provos, if they follow this advice, would become so popular that they would lose. How? Simply because, if we gave in, they would stop all this exquisite public service and settle down to build grim bungies in Neath and claim EC grants, and that we cannot have, not at any price.

17

IONCE LIVED briefly in a flat which had been occupied by a wicked organist come to no good. I could tell because there were regular deliveries of child pornography addressed to him. 'B. Mus. LRCM FRCO' it said after his name on the label, and what sort of person recites his professional qualification when ordering nasty smut? A wicked organist, I suppose.

We make more fuss about prostitution and pornography in this country than anywhere else in the world, despite the fact that we don't have any. There's nowhere in London where you can buy a copy of *Ero The Swedish Orgy Magazine*, FRCO or no FRCO. (Although there are plenty of places willing to sell you stuff *masquerading* as *ETSWOM* but which turns out to be full of black-and-white photographs of black and white Romford shopgirls splayed on Mr David Sullivan's vulgar black and white sofa. You aren't supposed to find out until you take the Sellotape off at home when the wife has finally found her specs and gone out.)

Yet week after week people stand up on their hind legs and drivel about the menace of pornography ('degrading . . . rape . . . menace to society') and prostitution ('male attitudes . . . degrading . . . menace to society') although they might as well be talking about the menace of polar bears running wild through Wolverhampton.

It's all nonsense. I am all in favour of wild filth and hookers but nobody else has got the nerve to admit it, and we all listen to these imbecile women and the craven men who grease up to them in the hope of a poke.

What we should *really* ban is *Which* magazine. It comes through my letterbox once a month (although it seems much more often) on the premise that my long-departed predecessors in this joint once sent off a coupon and forgot to countermand the bankers' order. Usually I send it back

55

with DEAD written on the front, but this time I opened it.

I wish I hadn't because it presented me with such a picture of human degradation and despair as you could not hope to encounter in my entire collection of *Ero The Swedish Orgy Magazine*, and probably not if you were to spend a whole fortnight down at the Royal College of Organists' library in your pedalling shoes and your Buxtehude-style mac. I imagine its readers are the sort of awful couples in jerseys who write in to *That's Life*. They have names like Heather and Malcolm. They budget. They make appointments with each other for sexual intercourse ('I think I can fit you in on Friday') and go on little trips to shop around for carpet deodorisers ('Banish nasty pet odours') and send off for the Franklin Mint Classic Car Collection ('Actual size 0.3 mm') and wear Hunter boots and *Daily Mail* special offer Barbour-style coats. They squirt Alpine Meadow Haze *before* they have a shit, in case they offend themselves by Smelling Something Unnecessary.

Oh God but it is awful beyond the power of the human pen. There is no vocabulary to describe its obsessional, hypnotic ghastliness. The editor is called Sue Leggate and signs her column in the sort of writing you'd expect someone called Sue who is the editor of *Which* to have, and straight away one is plunged into a veritable Saturnalia of wild living. Return your Morphy Richards 44210 if the batch number of the gold 'tested' label is between 0189 and 2089! Drive a hard bargain if you suspect your 'new' car has been pre-registered! Insurance Choice from the TSB makes little effort to establish whether or not people need life insurance! Do be careful buying goods on Access in Korea! Swimming pools can be DIRTY! We put another 29 compact cameras through their paces to bring you RIGHT UP TO DATE on what's in the shops . . .

Pausing only to point out that people have been widdling in swimming pools for generations and the only compact camera worth buying is the Leica M6, let's think about fuzzy logic. The new generation of computer software will probably have algorithms designed to get the right answer almost all the time. Not always. Bugs in the software, usually introduced in the pursuit of that elusive *always*, mean that even software that *always* gets it right will go bang sooner or later, probably with far more serious (because unpredictable) results than the software which contentedly *usually* gets it right.

The urge to get it *always* right is a killer. The more you try to stay safe and prevent anything going wrong, the more terrible the thing which happens, as it is bound to eventually, will be. The toaster won't catch fire but the house will explode due to rogue terrorists driving past with a dangerously unstable nuclear device. The car salesman's wife will be having an affair, he will be in trouble with American Express, his haemorrhoids will be playing him hell and instead of knocking off £100 he will go barking mad and kill you. The stuff you pay cash for in Korea will turn out to be filled with heroin which will be detected at the airport and six months later you will face a firing squad. You will drown in the crystal-clear water of the *Which*-approved swimming pool. Your compact camera will be fine but you will get the wicked organist's films back by mistake and Heather will inform the police before running off with Geoff, the ne'er-do-well so-called 'rock guitarist' from number 63.

It doesn't work. *Which* encourages people to think they can keep life's ghastliness at bay, with the effect that what eventually happens to them is ghastly beyond belief. Though it serves Malcolm and Heather right, this is a caring society, and the charitable status of the Consumer Association should be immediately revoked and its foul and corrupting publications banned (and while we are at it, let's beat Cecil Parkinson to a pulp and choke Gummer with the bleeding remains, eh?).

18

THIS IS THE LIFE. A spot of work in the cool of the morning, then out in the Provençal sunshine with a long cool something. Just knock this column off, half an hour, then the day is my own. The only cloud on the horizon is the *poubelle* or, rather, the cloud of flies around the *poubelle*, because it's full up and the frightfully clever little chute down which you throw stuff from the kitchen work surface is bunged up and the frightfully clever little maggots are crawling up and out of the frightfully clever little chute and on to the work surface.

So better do something about that, then just knock this column off. The sun is coming along nicely: round these parts it goes up over the yard-arm with an almost audible click at around 9.15 am.

My only problem is the water man who has come to deliver the water, which is what you would expect, except he wants a tip and I haven't got any money because I only had 19p when I suddenly decided to come here and, well, you know how travelling eats up the funds, I am down to 7p now and dependent on the kindness of strangers. I think on balance the water man can whistle for his tip and therefore I will whistle for my water but that wouldn't be so bad if there were any cigarettes. There are no cigarettes and for some reason you can't get cigarettes here except at the *tabac*.

That is my only problem, but it is not much of a problem. All I have to do is get to the *tabac* before noon, when it shuts for lunch, but I can't because the bastard has gone off in his car because I broke it when I turned it on to go to the *tabac*. It ran out of oil, although it was apparently fine when the water man came the first time, around dawn, just before the jets came over. The jets are not a problem, but the oil was. What irony. Dying for a smoke because of the water man. If he hadn't arrived with his lorry of water, the bastard wouldn't have had to move the car, thus using the last bit of oil, and then the red light wouldn't have come on until I was well on my way to the *tabac*. I could have said: 'Sod it, might as well carry on,' and carried on; the money difficulty we'll deal with when the time comes.

But apart from that, no problems. All I have to do is knock out this stuff, then my time is my own, out in the sun with something cool in a long glass, something short in a long glass, as it happens, because there'll be nothing to dilute it with on account of the water man is going to come back and wants his tip and he won't be able to have it so he'll probably suck all the water out of the water tank again. Probably got a colleague round the corner with an empty water lorry and a sucker against that very eventuality, but never mind.

No problems. Apart from the telephone men. They turned up hot on the heels of the water man while I was dealing with the oil problem and the frightfully clever maggots in the *poubelle*. This was the original telephone man and a new assistant, not the private telephone man with the reliable moustache who came to replace the original private telephone man with the unreliable moustache. He had been counter-manded by M Urbaniak's burglar alarm man who said the telephones were fine, which is exactly what the original public telephone man said.

But that was before the swimming pool man came to sort out the electric dog, which wasn't. The wires had gone, he said, which gave the original private telephone man something to think about, except he didn't know which. Nor did the original public telephone man, who . . . sorry? It's obvious. It paddles around the bottom of the pool eating leaves, hence 'electric dog'. A child of five could have worked that out, which is more than the swimming pool man could have. Or the original public telephone man.

It was the garden man who discovered the problem while he was looking for water. 'Can't use that,' he said, peering into the swimming pool. 'Who'd be a lizard, eh? A dog's life,' and then went into the bit under the dovecote where the pump is and said: 'Look – telephone wire's completely oxidised. What a shitty job. The whole job is shit. What shit put this shit in, eh? Never known weather like it.'

'The whole place is falling apart,' said the vineyard man. 'And if you think they are going to pipe water in from the town, you're mistaken.'

The telephone men, on the other hand, were more hopeful. Hopeful about the water, that is. The telephones were a different matter. They arrived in two vans but forgot their spanner and went off in a huff saying everything was fine and if we wanted to complain, the second private telephone man with the reliable moustache was the one to complain about.

They supposed he thought he was clever but they knew better. Anyway, the second public telephone man's wife had been to Nice only last week and it was a whorehouse and no good would come of it. So they went off in a huff and rang up just now to say they had made some adjustments and there was probably still a frying noise on the fax line and I said, yes, there is, and they said, there you are then, that's telephones all over for you.

Apart from that, no problems. I'll just belt this down the non-working fax line then my time's my own; out by the cracked pool among the lizards in the drought with the dead electric dog, a cigarette end falling from my lips and igniting the tinder-dry vineyards as I fall unconscious from sunstroke because the stove burnt the peak of my Jack Daniels hat. This is the life, you poor dumb bastards, this is the life.

19

ALL THAT NOBLE hawk-eyed sons of the desert stuff is just so much noble hawk-eyed sons of the desert stuff. Everyone knows that the Arabs won't do. It's not just the noble hawk-eyed sons of the desert stuff. It's the robe stuff and the big noses stuff, the broken-down taxis stuff and the shouting stuff and the holding hands stuff, not to mention the berks in green uniforms stuff and the rubber-stamp stuff. The best thing that could happen is for them all to invade each other simultaneously, all claim to have won, then shut up and sulk in that sort of boastful way that Arabs do best.

It's some time since I was last interrogated in a Kuwaiti jail but I did spend two years recently living on the Edgware Road so I know what I'm talking about. You can't found a culture on shambling about and Mercedes-buying and anyone who says otherwise is suffering from relativism; the Americans may think that is a good thing and believe we are all as good as each other, but they have got confused between relativism and relativity, the latter being a good idea which they haven't got the hang of and the former being a bad idea which they have, just as in so many other aspects of American life.

Washing, for example. Americans seem to wash all the time but they never really get clean, whereas the French never wash and never get clean either. And how come American water is so powerful? Stick an American shower in an English bathroom and our water would just be intimidated and turn tail, skulking back to the reservoir in its brown suit and puffy shoes, nurturing its grievance for the tea break. Which they don't have in America, the electricity being so weak. I suppose all the strength is used up in the water. You can fill a kettle in half a second in America but you could be dead before the bugger boiled.

But that, like so much else, is neither here nor there. The Arabs wash in sand and it's no good telling me that the buggers invented mathematics. They didn't, not these Arabs; the ones who invented mathematics were from the civilised coastal regions who spent their time thinking about the universe and wouldn't know a tent if it was up them sideways. They were totally different from the desert ones, who simply hung around in black tents and weren't astronomers at all; when they looked at the stars they just thought: hello, still there then, makes a change from sand, just like the Edgware Road ones look in the window of the gold-plated Mercedes accessory shop and think: want one of them, makes a change from sand.

Call that culture? Phooey. And it's no good pointing out that we gave the world Isaac Newton, inventor of the cat flap, and Stephen Hawking, who has yet to come up with anything half as useful, but on the other hand managed to write a best-selling book and change the way we think about absolutely everything. But it's no basis for a culture, not a *culture*, a real one, the Lady Antonia Pinter sort where everyone sits around saying, 'Oh apsley I do so agree there is a sort of linearity about his later work, almost a sort of alert and toroidal flatulence'. Astrophysics now is just a complicated way of saying: hello, still there then, makes a change from sand, except that we're more sophisticated than the Bedouin in that we say: mind you, don't count on it, it'll all turn back to sand in the end, you mark my words.

I am anxious to learn the secret before the universe collapses upon itself and everything turns back to huge sand, which could be sooner than we think. Sooner, actually, than *you* think, since I think it will be sooner than you do.

I mean, I know about this stuff. I was there. When the Kuwaiti sods got me and Albrecht on account of the jeep being camouflaged but not quite well enough, they completely ignored our forged diplomatic credentials and put us in jail. Three jerry cans of illicit alcohol might not seem much to you but there was a bit of local trouble about a Scottish pilot who had reneged on a complex deal involving illegal tortoise-running via a Japanese lesbian middle-woman in Muscat, so tempers were short. We finally got out after a complicated barter involving my mirror-lens Ray-Bans, three back-issues of a Danish art publication called *Teenage Sex* and the seizure of our jerry cans, but not before being interrogated all night.

The interrogation was grim. They sat us in a small concrete room illuminated by a bare light-bulb and then repeatedly apologised at us because the Calor gas had run out so there was only cold stuff for supper. Then we were subjected to political indoctrination. 'Those Iraqis,' they said, 'are buggers. One day they'll be across the border in a pack. They've got all the stuff, you know: jeeps, tanks, bazookas, the lot.' 'What about you?' said Albrecht. 'Oh, we've got all the stuff too, but look at how we live. We're the army, you know. Would you call that a decent dinner? No, when the Iraqis come across the border, that's it. You know how many of them are in the army?' 'No,' we said. 'All of them. The whole bloody country is in the army, and what's more, they're nicking our oil. Okay. Give us the dirty books and go away.'

That is the sort of person we are dealing with here. If you think the Iraq/Kuwait conflict is just a little local difficulty you are mistaken. It could be the end of civilisation. We could all end up running cut-price surgical stores in Vietnam and all the gold Mercedes accessories and quantum gravitational theorems in the world won't help. Our only chance is to get someone like Berthe Milton to flood the place with mucky books and buckshee tortoiseshell before things get really difficult.

20

I CRAWLED BACK into this decaying hell-hole of a 'country' last week but I shall not be staying for long. It's chaos. I can't even ring up my enemies for solace because British Telecom (it's *who* they answer to, precisely?) have disconnected my lines for payment of the bill. Payment *twice* actually: once in my absence, and once on my return, which flung them into complete confusion to the extent that joke 'engineers' in plastic trousers were despatched into the exchange to seize my equipment and throw it away.

This won't do. The gas people can whistle for a bit – one can get by on charcoal and it's actually a relief not to have gas around the place; I can run away again next week without worrying about the house blowing up – but the telephone is essential. The only reason I returned was to try to regain the affections of the woman I love, and intermittent, crackling communications from traffic-haunted, kebab-reeking telephone kiosks fail to carry the subtext of wealth and power that bimbos of her kidney seem to require before they will, let us be frank, put out for a chap. Nor can I communicate with my primary fallback, the erudite and *vicieuse* lady from Paris, since I cannot recall her address and even the French post office has proved unable to deliver a billet-doux addressed to The Woman With The Big Hat And The Holland & Holland Handcuffs. She Hangs Out In The 14th Arondissement, You'd Probably Catch Her At Lipp or Les Deux Magots, Oh For God's Sake, You Know Who I Mean.

And so (it's at times like this you need an admiral, and a surgeon called Farquarson and old Bollocks the waiter, clustered around the fireside) began the adventure which led to my identifying the fabled Arsehole of the Universe. It left me scarred and I will never be able to hear *Swan Lake* without screaming, rolling my eyes, and beating an old lady to death (I always carry an old lady, next to the mug shot and the lariat). But was it worth it? That, reader, is for you to say, though if you think I give a pig's foot about your opinion you must be even more barking mad than I thought.

When you ring up British Telecom, the first thing is that they don't answer. Then you try again and they do. This is a good trick. A woman – her voice strained by snobbery and vaginismus – thanks you for calling and tells you you'll have to wait. That is something I have heard on innumerable occasions, but at least the women who usually deliver the line have the courtesy to launch immediately into insane self-justifications about finding out who they really are, having been hurt in the past, suffering from insurmountable insecurity, being already committed to dog-breathed backbenchers and finding me so physically repulsive and mentally overpowering that their flesh creeps at the very thought of my name.

British Telecom don't do this. They simply play *Swan Lake* at you while the Phonecard bleeds its thin magnetic life into the slot. After a few hours of this I realised that the only way to survive was to find Mr Iain Vallance, British Telecom's profoundly unattractive 'boss', and disembowel him slowly with the Nantucket flensing knife I always carry next to the mug shot, the lariat and the old lady. That proving impractical, regular irrigation was the next best thing, and over the last week you could have seen me at all hours of the day, huddled in a pre-vandalised phone booth outside Nabeel's Tandoori, swigging raw Pimm's from the bottle and alternately cuffing and consoling a small female in an orange dress who claimed to be my daughter.

When *Swan Lake* became too much to bear, I would call the woman I love, because being snarled at is better than being ignored, and there were even times when I wanted to ring up the dark-haired beauty who ruined my life and tell her that all I asked was for us to be reunited; but fortunately anything strong enough to twist the intellect to that pitch of craven supplication is banned in this country, just like everything else is banned in this country, which is why I am leaving at Christmas FOR EVER.

Presently, I got through to a woman in Accounts, who referred me to a woman in Sales, who referred me to Debt Management, who referred me to a woman in Accounts, who referred me to Customer Service, and eventually it became clear that the only thing to do was to go to Croydon, where their offices are.

And that, gentlemen, is how I discovered the legendary Arsehole of the Universe, a sort of reverse Shangri-La where you age hundreds of years in a mere lunchtime. Can I speak of the mystical Telecom eyrie, the fabled Delta Point, with its solemn procession of whining, impotent, bearded men in brown terylene suits? Can I tell of its burger bars, car parks, building society offices? Is my pen capable of painting its atmosphere of municipal snivelling and cheeseparing rapaciousness? Have I the tongue to sing its one-way system?

No.

The telephone is still not working, the woman I love is coming to be fed this evening and I have nothing to give her but blood, toil, tears and unpaid bills, my parents are disappointed in me but none of this is why I am leaving. I simply cannot countenance remaining in a country which can harbour a place like Croydon, and, despite the evidence of self-knowledge which allows them to erect Delta Point, I have to go. Sorry about that. But I'll be in touch. You'll find me near the Panthéon. Just follow the sound of clanking chains and whistling bullwhips.

21

OUT OF KILTER, out of cash, out of sorts but back in town again. Sing tra-la-la: *great green gobs of greasy, grimy gopher meat, and I forgot my spoon.* I have brought shame on the family (or was it disgrace? I cannot remember) and there is still no gas: it is paying the bill that does it. For years I never paid the bill and there was always gas, except when the mattressman burnt down the Lebanese bomb-factory but that was just a blip on the radar of my soul.

Now I pay the bills and there is no gas. Plus . . . I sit here with a fictional wimp, a popsy and a dwarf, getting nowhere. I no longer know what love is or what it can do, but there is a woman in Paris who wants me to whip her to the *Liebestod*. If the price of joy is traumatic deafness and a forearm like Arnold Schwarzenegger, so be it. I have my train ticket in my pocket and eat a spoonful of Conolly's Hide Food every morning and soon I shall be gone for good.

There is little to stay for. They cleaned me out the other day. I went to the bank for my Monday morning experience of ritual humiliation (if I am going to take up sadomasochism it seems only fair to learn to take it as well as dish it out) and they were up the ladder before you could say 'Don't get involved'. Everything gone except the damned manuscript. I could have done with a change of excuse. You can only leave a novel at Granny's so often and the dog has eaten it twice in the last three months.

I didn't notice at first, just came back smarting and sat down to recalculate my overdraft. Then I noticed the television was missing. I thought: probably a practical joke. The street below was seething with fluorescent Lycra boogies on skateboards, just the sort to play practical jokes: *hey, let's break in and take all the Leicas and the television and the tape recorders and stuff and make him think we STOLE it! Yo!*

But it couldn't have been them. They have been educated by the Enterprise Society and would be unable to hack the complex ladder technology; working out how to go up it and difficult stuff like that. The place is surrounded by grilles and locks and electric gates, so the burglars got in through the bedroom window. I always said that stuff was a waste of money.

Still, it's a relief. The policeman said he expected that I felt violated, but he was wrong. I know about violation and it doesn't feel like this at all. This just feels like being burgled. We're good at feeling that, here. Good at words, too: burgle, burglar, burglary. The Americans go about it differently: burglar, burglarize, burglarization. Maybe they'll move on, soon, and we'll have burglarizationeers who burglarizationize us, leaving us victims of burglarizationeerage. Whatever, it's another layer of insecurity peeled away. No need to worry about them getting the Leicas because they've already got the Leicas. They didn't get the harpsichord but I suppose they'd have looked conspicuous. You might think there was something a bit conspicuous about walking around Clapham laden with a ladder, six cameras, a flying jacket and a television, but they are not-quite-yuppies around here, they don't like to get involved, didn't see a *thing*, how awful, O how apsley *horrid*. Too busy worrying about parking spaces, I suppose.

And that's another reason I can't stay here. I lured the woman I love here the other day for a hot snail supper (my father never told me that a woman who will eat snails will do *anything*, and he was quite right: they won't) and had got to the three-bottle stage of pitching some fairly lacy woo, with matching accessories, when the people across the courtyard went tumultuously mad about her car being in their *special space*. The row which followed was entertaining but destroyed my campaign, which had just reached the Jordan-closes-its-borders stage. So, fired up by a lethal combination of testosterone, frustration, snail and chemical weaponry (bought by the case from the off-licence round the corner), I surged out like

68

a fat dishevelled sort of absolute vortex and went critical, returning to find the damned woman crouched on the stairs with a daft sort of my-hero expression on her 'face'.

Well, we can't have that. I've been down the my-hero route before and it ends in contempt, they are disappointed in you, do you call yourself a man, that sort of stuff. Never again. I could transfer my desires to the woman across the courtyard who now thinks I am a monster and came round, trembling, the following morning to supplicate, but I don't think I can be bothered. Flagellation and Wagner in the *quatorzième* seem much more appropriate and, who knows, I may be able to escalate things from mere horsewhips. I have been reading the catalogues and it's all bridles and handcuffs, martinets and saddle-soap, nothing to indicate that we have moved out of the 18th century at all. I think I shall surprise her with an outburst of sadomasochistic *amour fou* echoing the technological spirit of the times. A big aluminium Halliburton Zero case containing a few Sarin and VX warheads and a recoilless wire-guided rocket launcher would do the trick, or maybe just a simple bazooka at point-blank range: the pleasure would be transient but intense and she would remember me with affection for the rest of her life.

God knows what's in it for me, but anyone who thinks that human relationships are a source of mutual comfort and security is welcome to take the reins of the life I am leaving behind me. They'll get the shock of their life but on the other hand there'll always be somewhere to park, which is what really counts (unless you're incognito on the left bank with a fistful of leather and an earload of *Tristan und Isolde*, ho ho).

22

THE AIR ITSELF now has become more angular, the soft curves of summer attenuating towards a hint of autumnal shrewishness, the climate turning bitter like a bad marriage. Isn't this a particularly fine style of writing wouldn't you say now? We are quite the literary gent this morning, but not thanks to any of you lot. School is back and the road is teeming with pallid, hooting, spotty teenagers and gigantic boogies in ludicrously complicated impotence shoes, up to no good. London's women have gone on diets and the wagon, deliberately mortifying their flesh and mine too. People are thinking about central heating: *not time to turn the heating on yet* they think, and go upstairs to get a jersey. We are regretting the Panama hats we bought to protect our pineal glands from the sun.

Soon it will be the endless evenings, fraught with old, thin memories of Bovril and Sooty, wet streets, lighting-up time, tentative girlfriends gone away to university, beer and colds, waiting outside Halfords for the number 29 bus, melancholy nights with headlights making patterns on the bedroom wall. Autumn is a Sunday evening indefinitely extended. It is the season of the provinces, bedsits in Sheffield, Cardiff sea-mists, raincoats and station platforms, desolation and loss.

But for me, autumn is a good time. Millions of you write in at this time of year to complain about your love-lives, writhing in your self-inflicted anguish. This cheers me up no end, particularly as so many of you disclose the identity and location of your romantic attachments. You fools. For me, this is a season of endless possibilities and mayhem. Armed with powerful hashish and my old straw hat, I stalk the land. You may wonder what you have done to deserve such pain but I shall make it worse. Yet I am a kindly person at heart and want you to be happy. Uncle Wiggly-Woggly's Advice For The Lovelorn. Complete in one exciting episode. All you need to know: Lights; action; Kleenex . . .

Dear Uncle Wiggly-Woggly: I have been hopelessly in love for four years with the most wonderful woman in creation, an angel, magical in form and spirit. She is an enchantress and has me under her spell. I can neither eat nor sleep and all my thoughts are of her. Yet she seems indifferent to my advances. Why is this? What can I do?

Well . . . it's because she doesn't fancy you, and there's nothing you can do about it, so grow up and stop feeling sorry for yourself. Take up fishing.

Dear Uncle Wiggly-Woggly: I'm sorry, I don't think you understand. I mean, she likes me. We go out to dinner a lot and she makes me laugh and she always seems pleased to see me, but we just can't, er, seem to, um, you know, get it together. I have tried fishing. The worms gave me the willies.

The correct phrase is 'get it on'. The reason you can't is that she doesn't fancy you. The reason you goes out to dinner with you is that women like to eat, too. The reason she's pleased to see you is because she likes you. The reason she makes you laugh a lot is because you are over-excited about the possibility of boffing her. This is an error. If she has not let you boff her after four years, she is never going to. Ever. This is a fact. Assimilate it, then see if the ratbag makes you laugh. Fly-fishing does not involve worms.

But I love her. I adore her. And I think she does fancy me. I just think she daren't admit it, because she knows it would lead to deep water and she's scared of making a commitment, you know? And anyway she's had a rough time recently and I think she probably just wants to, er, find her, um, space, you know, kind of, er, lick her wounds. And if you think I am going to hang around up to the waist in icy water surrounded by horrid Japanese businessmen, you must be barking mad.

Stop saying 'but . . .' Your case is hopeless. None of that stuff matters. You don't adore her at all. If you adored her you'd be happy. What you adore is the idea of what it might be like if she'd let you boff her. Are you mad? If anything was going to happen it would have done by now. It hasn't, and it won't. Count your blessings. I am not barking mad, but I think you are. How about hunting?

But I am good to her. I pay for everything. I take care of my appearance and am always immaculate when we meet. I compliment her a lot and am chivalrous and attentive. I also hate horses and am agoraphobic.

This will not help if she doesn't want you. If she did want you, you could turn up penniless, drunk, in cracked sunglasses and a crumpled suit, unshaven, having not slept for three days, ignore her altogether apart from the occasional snarl, and next thing you know she would be covering your upturned face with burning kisses. I would suggest you try dignity or, failing that, rape.

Dear Uncle Wiggly-Woggly: I have tried dignity and it didn't work. Nor did chivalry, machismo, sensitivity, wistfulness, domination, lechery, skittish flirtatiousness, hard-faced froideur, romanticism, casual effrontery and crawling like a worm. I have tried rape. That didn't work either and I still do not know what to do. I get hay fever.

You need not do anything. She will never speak to you again and, furthermore, nor will any of your friends. Two big blue incorruptible policemen will shortly arrive at your door and carry you off to a cell where you can pass a cosy few years with some nice new friends and make a fresh start. Hobby suggestions: learning to roll very thin cigarettes and handling multiple violations by huge GBH practitioners.

23

ELLO, HONEY, LOVELY to hear from you. Fine you know, can't complain. Things are . . .

Well, yes, apart from that. How did you come to hear about it?

Did he? Did he? Well let me tell you he's not to be trusted, came over here in a frightful state, reeking of Old Crow and started dismantling the . . .

No, that's true, I hadn't actually paid for it, but that's not the point, there are proper processes of law for this sort of thing and I don't think coming in here like Rambo and frightening the children with his . . .

So? If there had been any children here, they would have been frightened, and that's what counts unless you are one of these – what are they? logical positivists? Anyway I told him where to get off, I said: 'You can take your mole wrench and get the hell out of here, move slowly towards the door or I'll snap your neck off, you reeking blowhard.'

No, well, not in those words exactly. But that was the gist.

I did. I did. What did he say?

Oh, did he now? I see. I rather take exception to that. Hiding in the bedroom indeed. I did nothing of the sort. I may have gone there, there's nothing cowardly about going to the bedroom in my own house, I presume, unless . . .

All right, going to the bedroom in the house in which I live, just because I haven't fallen into the ridiculous obsession about home-ownership doesn't mean . . .

Oh? Well, for your information, that sort of stuff is supposed to be confidential and you are probably committing a criminal offence just listening to it, and anyway the Northern Rock Building Society is only one among thousands. I could get a mortgage if I wanted to, just like that.

That's nothing to do with it. I simply choose not to use

them. If you can't pay cash on the nail, go without, that's what I always say.

Well, it's what I always say now. This credit business is responsible for more human misery than anything else, and as for the foolish status display of gold credit cards, it's really pathetic. I . . .

That is arrant nonsense. I didn't buy the Giorgio Armani jacket simply because I decided on mature reflection that I had no need of that sort of prop to bolster my ego, and if she wouldn't give me a . . .

Yes, the salesman did cut up my gold card, you are quite correct, but only because it was out of date. He cut it up at my request. There is no point in walking around with an out-of-date card in your pocket. I have no doubt they would have sent me a new gold card three weeks before the old one expired, except that I informed them that I would not be requiring one.

Yes I did. Yes I did. What's got into you, anyway?

That is nothing to do with me. I'm sorry but you can't pin that on me. It's probably something just going around, it's probably nothing, it's probably just stress, antibiotics will clear it up in no time, nothing to do with me at all.

Why? What is there to talk about? As far as I'm concerned I know exactly where things stand. I don't see any point in dragging myself across London to some terrible poncey bar full of pimps and berks just to listen to . . .

I am not scared. Why should I be scared?

Well, yes. I am scared of being shot. By my godson.

Oh, I see. I'm being grotesquely ridiculous am I? Have you never heard of anyone being shot by his godson before? Let me tell you, this man has it in for me, he thinks I have got the woman he loves clad in tight black latex and chained to the burglar grilles.

I am most certainly not a pervert. I happen to believe that the sexual act is the most powerful channel of communication available to us, not some beastly and brutal act of . . .

74

Really? Well, it wasn't for me, either, and not for want of trying, so don't think a couple of miserable silk scarves and a bicycle pump give you any insight into me, you know nothing about me at all, you just think you do.

What do you mean, and another thing?

What is pathetic about that? I'm simply being realistic, you may think you are the only one with a grudge but you are mistaken. I don't know what's wrong with you people anyway, if I had known things were going to turn out like this I would never have bothered, months of aggravation and misery and for what? Eh? For what?

Apart from that.

What woman? There isn't a woman, it must be a crossed line, it's the cleaning woman.

Yes, I know she usually comes on Tuesdays but today she has come today. Is there something wrong with that?

Oh. Oh, I *see*. You heard her say 'Come upstairs, honey, I've found the key to the handcuffs.' So *that's* what she said, is it? I thought she said, er, er, I thought she said, er . . .

So you think I am the sort of person who has people handcuffed in the middle of a working day, I mean, pardon me for asking, you're not in collusion with my godson are you by any chance? I should think the two of you will get on pretty well together, you are both barking mad, perhaps I should be the one doing some shooting round here, perhaps a few ounces of lead between the eyes would make you . . .

So? I could get a gun. If I wanted to. Just like that.

24

I HAD THOUGHT, earlier this week, about becoming a New Man but now I have changed my mind. Not that I am incapable. I can do all that stuff and the outlay is nugatory. All you need is soft hands and a jersey and everyone loves you. It could be utterly life-enhancing. I could go to therapy groups and really come to empathise with the problems of women in a male-dominated society and maybe after a while I would become confident of my own identity as a *person*, don't you see, oh yes I do understand, we are all in this together it is the only world we have, please do not see me as threatening.

The trouble is, I rather like being threatening. I like seeing people's faces shrivel up when I come into the room, I like getting angry telephone calls from their friends ('She has been in floods of tears for hours and I just want you to know that everyone else may let you get away with it but I think you are a complete shit, you may think it's clever but all I can say is you are going to end up a very lonely bitter and twisted little old man') and hearing that people have emigrated to get away from me. Perhaps it is my reptile blood but the reunification of Germany filled me with rage at the sight of all those happy tearful Huns and if I ever come across anyone else being nice about gorillas I shall kill them. The brute creation has it all mapped out nicely and anyone who thinks we owe these buggers anything is completely wrong. 'There's no harm in chimpanzees,' they will tell you. 'Man is the only animal that kills more than it needs to eat,' but they have obviously never seen a pack of chimpanzees rip a colobus monkey to pieces and play tag with the remains. Neither have I, as it happens, but that is simply because I do not spend my precious spare time hanging around a lot of beastly monkeys with no conversation who never buy their round. I'd rather be here on my own, under the covers, thwarted and cross.

But most of all I think confrontation is the thing. I was talking to someone yesterday who was the last soldier in the British Army to be shot by a musket. I find that admirable. I want to be shot by a musket, too. I want to stride the desert sands, sneaking up a wadi with a platoon of thugs and a semi-automatic. I want to grow stubble and not change my underwear for weeks, and smell and swear a lot and kill people and not give a damn about it. There is limited scope for this sort of thing in London but the quality of life here is so appalling that it will be guerrilla warfare before long and we all ought to start preparing for it. The Bargepole Urban Commandos will be on the move by Christmas so watch your step.

First target will be fashionable media restaurants. Any-where which has ever served even the teensiest slice of pan-fried pigeon breast nestling in a lightly dressed salad of rocket and frisée will find us inexplicably in the kitchen, widdling in the stockpot and taunting the chef. Worse treat-ment will be meted out to anywhere which has ever served George Michael, especially if the staff affected not to notice him. In these cases we will tie them to their winsomely Gothic chairs and take over the stereo system, destroying the CDs of Vivaldi and Pachebel's Canon (as if he only wrote the one, for heaven's sake; actually he wrote nothing else but canons, canon after canon after bloody canon, all of them rotten) and replacing them with *Richard Clayderman's Greatest Hits* on perpetual replay; when they are foaming at the chops and yellow fat is leaking from their eyeballs, we will stuff them piecemeal into their own woks and feed them to the chimpanzees.

Having thus isolated the grinning media dickheads we will forbear from machine gunning them in the streets, leaving them merely to starve and chatter in the gutters. No more evenings in the Groucho boasting about their latest series or who has asked them to be the new editor of what; they will simply have to get wet or go home, and we will turn our attention to the bankers, starting with the man who said that Mr Ronson was, in his view, the finest businessman of today and his credit rating would in no way be affected by a conviction. This is rebarbative and shameless enough even in isolation but when seen in the light of my own experiences, the National Westminster Bank having seen fit to bounce a cheque for 35 quid and then charge me 30 quid for the privilege, becomes punishable only by slow death. My troops will be trained to debag these people and feed their shrivelled genitals into their own cashpoint slots before pressing the alarm button. And so it will go on. In the run-up to Christmas we will publicly disembowel anyone heard using the phrase 'in the run-up to Christmas'. Later, we will turn on you, and if we find you buying Christmas presents in Marks and Spencers we will creep up silently behind you and stuff tartan Pirelli slippers down your whining craw and douse you in cheap after shave until you reek to death. That will teach you the important lesson that it is not the thought that counts, but the present.

Finally, in a grand misogynistic Gala Night, we will capture any woman who has ever used the words 'It's not as easy as that, you have to give me time' and send her off to the vegetable cabarets of Patpong Road, where she will be exhibited for rental but find no takers at all until she finally expires of humiliation.

It is all going to be great fun and volunteers are welcome. And once we have cleaned up London, then we'll think about becoming New Men, but somehow I don't think there will be much demand.

25

WHAT A DELIGHTFUL week it has been, holed up above in the bed playing Passionate Sexual Intercourse on my own. I can't think what else to call it. Doctors And Nurses springs to mind, but that's already taken, though not by me, not all that often, and not without a fuss. They say a man is in his prime at 17 but between five and eight was my heyday as far as Doctors And Nurses were concerned. I was persuasive, ingenious and vigorous, and the girls were willing. Or possibly stupid. Perhaps it was just the innocent times in which we lived, halcyon days of sublime hopefulness, no cloud in the sunlit sky of pure existence, Europe ravaged by the war, the shadow of the Bomb, Macmillan creeping craftily up the margin and the Beatles naught but yolksuckers, still to hatch.

It all seems a long time ago and indeed it was. They probably don't even play Doctors And Nurses any more. They probably play Doctors And Barristers or Martina And Her Friend but whatever they call it let us hope the social workers don't find out or it'll be everyone into chokey straight off – special orders and private hearings before the judge, thin-lipped outrage beneath the dripping red noses and a cosy fug in Meeting Room 441 while Adrian, Nikki, Steve and Roz congratulate themselves on another job well done.

Then it's a quick call to the man from the evening paper and off for a celebratory tandoori. Why is it that any given Indian restaurant at any given time contains at least one table of social workers? And why are they such clichés? Roz is invariably the dumpy one with black-framed oval specs who seems to be entirely knitted out of scarves; she has a black bucket-bag in which she rummages and a clogged voice which sounds like something green trying to climb guiltily out of a drain. Adrian is the moody one with cropped hair and cheekbones who is Good With The Mums. 'Come on, love, it's not the end of the world' he says as the children are taken away. They think he looks like that what's-his-name the one on the telly; so does he and what an irony that he only chose social psychology because it sounded easy and would leave him lots of time for amateur dramatics. That alas didn't work out but at least he has small, greasy Steve as a foil.

Steve listens to the back-and-forth stuff about relationships, puts in his two penn'orth, is rebuffed ('God you're soanalyticall right Steve?') and wonders whether Roz will come back with him to listen to his Fairport Convention records.

And there is Nikki, ebony skin and a soft sweater like a flame, energy crackling off her. Nikki is keeping the plates warm on her own, the food is cranked up three or four spice-notches by her presence, you could warm your hands at her, she is the one who signs the papers, she is the one who sees the inverted crosses in the children's nightmares, she is the one for whom 'father' is cognate with 'buggery'.

Best to eat Chinese on a night like this, wouldn't you say, and hope that they don't notice. Best, above all, to stay in, playing Passionate Sexual Intercourse, just like me. How you do it is this: you have a small stroke, a touch of cancer, a bit of pleurisy, your right arm goes numb and your left foot tingles, your head hurts, your hair hurts, your chest sings like a calliope, and you go to bed. Then begins a rich and Victorian fantasy life of bed-ridden indolence.

The room itself should be cool, the bed warm. Every now and then you sit up and say 'Come along now Mr Bargepole, time for your medicine,' and eat some Night Nurse. In the early hours of the morning, you run a cool hand over your fevered brow (this column will supply cool hands upon request), murmur 'Dear, dear' and get out of bed, pretending to sit in the corner while you plump up the pillows and smooth down the sheets. Then you get back in and sink down in luxury. You can hallucinate any other aspects of the invalid life you wish: inexplicably delicious smells from the kitchen below; the murmur of grave consultants; people bringing chicken soup; hooves on muffled straw.

A lifetime could drift away providing Adrian, Nikki, Steve and Roz do not come by. 'Why is his light on,' they will think, 'he is probably buggering children just like all men, the bastard.' 'No no,' they will also think hurriedly, 'it is not his fault, he is the product of an uncaring society which forces men to suppress their emotions and will not let them cry.' Why it is so important that we cry I cannot understand, but when they come to get me, if it is that or pokey I will blub my eyes out like a trouper, and if all else fails I shall tell them about the network of secret tunnels beneath Wollaton Hall in Nottingham where I and a number of other six-year-old children were taken many years ago, long before all this Satanism stuff hit the inside pages. It was a strangely ritual and formalised occasion; we were led from the upper floors to the tunnels in a line, an adult in a uniform before and behind; our blood was chilled with stories of what had happened in the past and what would happen in the future were we not to comply. Skeletons were hinted at, gore and torture. We were chilled, chastened and our dreams haunted for months, and if Adrian, Nikki, Steve or Roz had got hold of us, the stories we would have told would have had them filling out in triplicate before you could say 'caring professionals'. I expect we'd have forgotten to mention that it was a special treat, organised for Nigel Kenworthy's birthday party and that we all had a hell of a good time, but there you are, that's social work. Passionate Sexual Intercourse is much, much safer.

26

A NUMBER OF disturbing things have come to my attention recently including the fact that jokes are being removed from this column by members of the editorial staff whose brains are curdled from hanging around the Groucho club waiting to see who I come in with, instead of getting on with their work. So that these fundamentally absurd people can continue with their drenched and sickly lifestyles instead of having to attend to irksome trivialities, I shall cut my own column from now on.

There was a good joke in there, but I cut it.

Another disturbing thing is that certain people who know precisely who they are have taken to reading this stuff in the hope of finding out what I am up to, where I am, what I am going to do about various things and what is going on in my mind. It has ever been my intention to promote human happiness wherever possible, so here is the inside poop, damn you. All you need to do is work out which bits apply to you. And, of course, which bits are true. Here you are, and I hope you all choke (although I mean that in a caring way). And as for the rest of you, you keep your snouts out of it. This is private. Go and read Koenig. She's good for you. And what a sex-bomb! Why, if I had half the chance, I'd . . . sorry. Here:

1. I am working on it at the moment. It's really just a question of final tidying-up. Actually I am quite pleased with the way it is going and I think you will be too. I'd love to have lunch with you, yes, but I'm kind of hunkered down at the moment so I'm simply not going out at all, as I am sure you will understand.

2. They haven't? The *bastards*. I shall get on to them straight away. What? No; there was plenty of money in the account; I paid in a big cheque only last week.

3. Oh what a shame. But my FiloFax is absolutely full for the next month.

4. I've been thinking about it and I've decided you were just fishing for a reaction. Well, I'm sorry: you're not going to get one. I made my feelings perfectly clear and if you chose to disbelieve me that's your privilege. Anyway it's too late now. There's such a thing as dignity you know. So horse-poo in the road and no returns, that's what I say. What do *you* say?

5. I've tried to call you umpteen times but you've been engaged. God knows what you do on the telephone. Are you running some sort of phone-sex business from home? If so, who for? And do you need a technical adviser?

6. Frankly, I think if anyone should be complaining about plagiarism, it's me. Frankly, I think you've got a nerve.

7. I *have* seen somebody about it. As a matter of fact I went yesterday. No, I *won't* tell you who it was. Because I won't.

8. Three, actually, but only one was collapsible. The other two were a bit slimy but I soon fixed that. I'll show you if you come round.

9. See 1.

10. I think I *do* love you. I think I loved you from the moment we first met. I know that sounds awfully corny but that's the truth.

11. I will have to have a word with my accountant; he's responsible for all that sort of stuff.

12. It wasn't actually cut off, a suggestion which, to be honest, I find rather offensive. It simply broke.

13. Pawn it? I certainly did not pawn it. It is being repaired. There are problems obtaining the spare parts, that is all.

14. See 1.

15. Of *course* I respect you. It's just that it was very late, I was tired, it was dark, I was wearing sunglasses, and for a moment I thought you were someone else.

16. I was perfectly honest with you from the word go.

I made the situation absolutely clear. I don't think you can reproach me for anything.

17. I think I was not entirely honest with you. I should have made the situation clear from the word go. You'd be within your rights to reproach me though I hope you won't.

18. It was certainly *not* past its sell-by date. I expect you just got one of those bugs that have been going around.

19. Stockholm, actually. Of *course* I didn't sleep with her. Or anyone else, for that matter. It never crossed my mind.

20. Oh, the same as the next man, I suppose: latex, leather, sadomasochism, group sex, extreme fetishism, exhibitionism, bondage, that sort of thing. Anything you care to name, frankly the more bizarre the better.

21. See 1.

22. Of *course* not; I do not hold with drugs in any shape or form.

23. A couple of grams twice a week should do the trick. And whatever you're having yourself, preferably laced with opium.

24. The whole idea is abhorrent, except in the context of a proper committed relationship. I want you to understand that.

25. What a nice idea. We could stay overnight, make a weekend of it.

26. Of course I don't mind. I absolutely understand that you need to water the plants and clean the birdcage. I'm quite happy on my own. Self-sufficient, that's me. Pine? Rubbish.

27. I think you should come clean. I can't live with this terrible secrecy any longer.

28. We're negotiating the final deal now so I should be able to pay you within the week.

29. Gone away: no forwarding address.

NOW IS THE SEASON of peace and goodwill but we all know what a lot of dogs' poop *that* is. You can forget goodwill for a start. Hands up everyone who isn't delighted every time a short, pushy, snipe-faced financier has his collar felt by the bogies and has to spend Christmas in pokey. See? Only other short, pushy, snipe-faced financiers. And the goodwill of a financier is like the purest bile of other men. The charges don't matter. Being a financier is enough. All you have to do is sneak up behind any of the buggers and murmur: 'The police are onto you,' and they're off like a shot, trembling in their Guccis, hiring men from Essex with Rottweilers and shredding documents.

There you are. So much for goodwill. It's either universal or it doesn't count. And as for peace, don't give me that stuff. Pulpits will be crammed from now until Hogmanay with shivering vicars snivelling about peace, but the truth is that we have far too much peace as it is. If we are to stand any chance at all, do you hear me, what we want is *less* peace and more violence. The clergymen with their cold noses and tiny willies won't tell you this because they know that, in any escalation of righteous violence, they will be the first to go, dragged from the ambo by red-faced men with creaky shoes and mail order anoraks, who will tread on their heads and break their pipestems. The Lord Thy God is a violent God and take no notice of the old baby-in-a-manger routine which is just a hackneyed old method of making everyone say 'Aaaah . . .' and then slipping it between the short ribs while the oafs are still cooing. Jesus may have been a baby once, but so was Roger Levitt and we aren't confused by *that*, not for a moment: sit tight, bide your time, let him grow up and then, *whop!*, slam the bugger in chokey and to hell with the weeping family.

But in the case of old Jesus, our eyes go all misty as though it is somehow evidence of God being not so bad after all, deigning to be incarnate as a little pudgy baby in the straw. This is just woolly thinking. If God wanted to take on human form, He had no option but to start off as a baby just like everyone else, and the simple fact is that He *is* so bad after all. Always was, always will be, *et in saecula saeculorum*. You can't help liking the bugger but that doesn't mean He's *nice*. He's not. He's shitty, unscrupulous, demonstrably violent from the word go and yet we were all fooled by the baby stunt. And every year we celebrate that neat bit of cradle chicanery by holding 'office parties' and thinking that the boss is 'quite human when you get to know him', because the sadistic, flat-eyed dork is on his best behaviour for one evening. The truth is that he *isn't* quite human really: he's quite horrid, really, and the quite-human-really bit is just a sop, permitting a further year – or, in God's case, an eternity – of violence, snarling, inexplicable mood changes and generally thinking of nobody except himself.

And what do we do? We suck up to the buggers and let them get away with it, thinking we are somehow following some dweeby, woolly-jersey example which they are blatantly *not* setting us. The fact is that the people who want us to be nice, from God right down to Mr Purgatroyd of Accounts, are all themselves unremittingly horrible. There's nothing we can do about God but we can sort out the rest of them if only we start thinking clearly about violence.

Let us start with a big-print example for the hard of thinking. What is the difference between (a) an act of violence against the civilians of a country with whom one is not at war, and (b) an act of violence against the civilians of a country with whom one is not at war? The answer, obviously, is: none whatever, and thus it is evident that there is no ethical difference between the Libyans blasting the hell out of Pan Am 103 and the Americans blasting the hell out of Tripoli. Once this point is understood, the way is clear for an explosion of healthy violence, and by 'healthy violence' I mean the use of unnecessary force against someone you hate on the sound moral basis that (a) unnecessary force is a damn fine thing to use against hateful people and (b) the best way of testing whether someone is hateful is to see if you hate them.

We can therefore have an end to the tortured liberalism which has made our lives a hell on earth and a return to the principle of unrestrained and savage personal vendettas which God Himself instituted. It would have been perfectly easy to make a planet in a nice, William Morris sort of way, but oh no. Instead we had volcanoes and meteors and dinosaurs and ice ages and all the rest of the savage exhibitionism in which God specialises. And He's gone on like that ever since. I personally think His treatment of Job was not only immature but unforgivable, but if that's the sort of universe He wants, He can have it.

It should be amusing. Next time a health authority 'spokesman' is 'unavailable for comment', we should go around and tear his lungs out through his mouth. Next time some frightful scribbler ventilates his fears about his masculinity in public, we should have him gang-raped in Piccadilly by six 20-stone transvestites. We can anticipate the walls of the House of Commons being drenched in blood like a cheap Spanish abattoir. There will be flayings, mutilations, burnings not only at the stake but anywhere there is a victim and a Zippo. That is the message this Christmas. Anyone who says it isn't can expect a bazooka up the arse. God bless us every one . . . and if you believe that you'll believe anything.

28

BUGGA–DA–BA, BUGGA–DA–BA, BUGGA–DA–BA, bugga–de–
bugga–de EE–AAW, roll opening titles and fade up on
the Tardis creaking and shuddering as we are mystically
transported back in time to face strange sights, blasted
landscapes and outlandish creatures doing battle. But we need
not worry. The Doctor is at the helm, if there is a helm.
Doctor who? Oh my chickabiddies, nobody knows: he came
from nowhere but knows everything and exerts this strange
influence; people find themselves voting for him without
knowing quite why . . .

What an extraordinarily English fantasy this has all turned
out to be. Overnight we have drifted back several decades
into a world of toast soldiers, Horlicks and Grandpa sleeping
by the fire. Soon it will be time to turn on the big light
and draw the curtains; Daddy will come in from raking up
the leaves as a soft autumnal mist drifts across the lawn.
We who were Thatcher's Children are become the Ovaltinies.

It's a curious nightmare, no less ghastly for going under
the guise of a cosy dream: everything will be all right now
that the Doctor is in charge: some say he came from a family of circus artistes, others that his home is Aldebaran, but
nobody really knows and nobody really cares. Like Arthur,
he has simply materialised from some ageless mire with
gleaming spectacles and phantom moustache to lead us, not
into a future of glorious battles and staunch endeavour, but
back into a comfortable past of woollies and toasted toes.

We have, like the Chinese curse, lived in interesting times,
and now we want dull ones; and so, by some mystic process
of electoral communion, we have chosen Doctor Who to lead
us gently backwards again. Of course the European nonsense
is just a blind. We are not Europeans nor do we wish to be.
We are a damp and marginal island, giggling as we sink; for

a decade we have been forced to pull ourselves together but the national character has now reasserted itself and, under the Doctor, we can all untense our muscles 'til they sag, sag, sag and wait until we drop down dead. True Europeans would never have selected the Doctor. The French, for example, would have chosen Heseltine. He would have appealed to them with his 'sophistical lamentations' (© M Foot 1990), his pompadour, his flashy wife and daughters, the naked hunger of his ambitions and the subtle air of the *tombeur* which hangs about him like a nimbus. But we could not have this driven entrepreneur; what would have attracted other nations repelled us: his country house, his mad staring eyes, his noticeable shirts, the indefinable sense that he sleeps upside down, hanging from a rafter. Nor could we have had Douglas Hurd. Charming, distinguished, a patrician and diplomatist, he would have pleased much of Europe but, to us, he had committed innumerable sins, chief of which was that he speaks posh. What's more, he's one of those writing johnnies and you can't trust writing johnnies. It starts with the odd paragraph here and there, but soon grows into whole, entire books, along with sleeping with women, drinking, not getting up in the morning and having thoughts. We do not hold with thoughts and as for writing novels, well: I've read a novel and it was blatantly obvious that the bastard was simply making it up.

What will do very nicely is Doctor Who, and that's who we've got. Goody. Even the *Daily Mail*, after a post-resignation edition of such drooling hagiography that the only appropriate reaction would be a giant erection (as if there is any other kind), responded to Doctor Who's election by saying It Couldn't Happen to a Nicer Man, which tells us all we need to know: that becoming Prime Minister is a spot of luck, a turn-up for the books, well I never, out of a clear blue sky, it goes to show, a nice hot cup of tea, it's *Muffin the Mule* on later, oooh luvverly, a nice blue serge from Montague Burton, a run in the Vauxhall, ten Woodbines please luv, *Brighton Rock*, no better than she ought to be, mind me roll-on, oooh you're all fingers and thumbs, 'ere, let me do it, a nice bottle of stout with a port in it, can't complain, hold tight now please, who does she think she is, time gentlemen please, mind you wrap up warm now, see you tomorrow then Flo, bye Elsie, ta-ra Flo, nightie-night, toodle-oo, g'night . . . And there will be no more oyster mushrooms, no more Alaïa frocks, no more copies of *The Fred*, no more cocaine; no more Bollinger, no more Manolo Blahnik come-fuck-me shoes, no more rock publicists in Gaultier sunglasses; no more Vodafones, no more Janet Street-Porter, no more arbitrage; no more Canary Wharf, no more junk fax.

Penetrative sex will make a comeback and we won't care how it was for them. We will know our place and make do. We won't reckon much to foreigners with their nasty lavvies and the mucked-about food cooked in jam. We will go to Skegness. We will come out on strike against these new-fangled ways. The darkies will be all right once you get to know them but we won't want our daughters to marry one. Our good overcoat will see us through and our car will get us from A to B. It will all be lovely, the misty English socialism of the Boulting Brothers. England, our England: a shield pillar-box gules, a macintosh passant, the crest privet with a policeman's helmet. Hooray! There's nothing for Labour to do now, of course, but we never held much with them anyway. There is no alternative. (Odd sense of *déjà vu* there for a moment, but it will pass. It always does.)

29

HAPPY NEW YEAR, you nebbishes. You coneheads. It won't do you any good at all. You may think it is time for a fresh start but that's all flim-flam and the after-effects of doing compulsory stir in the flabby bosom of your horrible families; of enforced generosity and big food; most of all, of drink. You have spent the last fortnight sucking the Hydra's blood, in the form of hateful cocktails and sweet sherry, gimlets, Banshees and Moscow Mules. Your giblets have been steeped in paraquat and your brains greased fatly so that, for weeks to come, you will stare glumly into your beer wondering vaguely why there isn't a paper umbrella and an unnatural cherry in it.

The resolutions of achievement to which you will even now be clinging pathetically are nothing more than the over-compensations of a sickened mind. As you waddle vertiginously towards your job you will be conscious, not of successes yet to come, but of lurchingly awful failures securely in the bag. Hence the absurd turning over of new leaves, which invariably reveals nothing but old creepy-crawlies beneath.

You see, I know your minds, and I know the little lists that even the wife of Derek Baxter from Corporate Planning (with whom you have been sleeping since the Torquay conference last July) doesn't know about. (1) Give up Tufty Baxter. (2) Get up an hour earlier every day. (3) Make an effort with family life. (4) No more fantasies about living alone in a Docklands loft. (5) Admit to liking Richard Clayderman. (6) Abjure pronography. (8) Earn £75k this year and take Tufty to Pattaya Beach for three-way orgy with big-breasted Siamese. (9) Learn to spell pronography. (8a) Maybe four-way orgy with big-breasted Siamese and small-breasted Siamese, why not? (10) Focus mind. No more dissipation of energies. (11) Take Tufty Baxter to Zeitgeist and buy her a latex corset and slave-girl manacles. (12) Concentrate on work. (PS) Dear God please don't let Olivia find out about Tufty Baxter and I promise I will give up all that stuff with fish . . .

Oh yes, I know. But do not be embarrassed and, above all, do not put these foolish ideas into practice. Like the poor stout-sodden Erse who believes he can hoist the entire British forces with a lashed-up petard of farm-grade stump dynamite, it is only the drink talking and will blow up in your face. Bide your time, take your hangover like a man, and before the middle of January you will be back to your old self, not in the sense of being about to die ('Good God, I saw him only last week and he was looking his old self . . .') but in the sense of being comfortably unambitious, clad in your awful grey suit, wasting your time talking nonsense with the colleagues (who, at the moment, you intend to trample all over in your fight to the top) and assiduously wearing Tufty Baxter down to a nub.

That's what real life is all about and the people who think otherwise are barking mad. Worst of all are the women. There's a sad place in Soho called Madame Jo-Jo's where the waitresses are all men, dressed up. They did fine business over Christmas, full of parties of sales clerks from Rumbelows and so forth, little men nudging each other and saying 'Bet you'd get a shock if you picked up one of them by mistake,' and, 'I don't know about the rest of them, but that one's definitely Julie Burchill.' For reasons I am not prepared to discuss, I visited this hellhole and for a while I thought that a transvestite might possibly be the answer. They are the only people left who are prepared to dedicate their lives to being women, after all. And, being blokes, they aren't horrible to us.

This is a disagreeable prospect. Horrible mad women are one of the great joys of life, and they are invariably much better in bed than the nice sort because their libidos are fuelled with high-octane rage. And what is wrong with their complaining that we are odious pigs? We *are* odious pigs. So, on the other hand, are they. When that sad man wrote in the *Sunday Times* the other day that women had to stop being so beastly, Kate Saunders responded the following week with a piece saying that he probably had a small willy.

My feelings precisely. No, it's the nice ones that are terrible, using their female charms in the pursuit of ambition. They are more distressing than any transvestite could ever be. I saw one the other day at her grim trade, charming everyone she could, twirling her beads and working the room. 'Who's that man?' 'That's Sir Florizel Bargepole.' 'Of . . . ?'

There you have it. 'Of . . . ?' It has all the naked status-hunting of an over-protective PA. The ageing pop fan Berkmann told me that when people's secretaries say 'Where are you calling from?' he replies 'Highgate, actually, but not the fashionable part, more sort of Archway borders.' If I had had my wits about me I would have told this grimly-networking bimbo that I was literary editor of *Beezer*, and then seduced her. The shock of sleeping with somebody who was no good for her career would probably have killed her, but far better to let her live. Soon she will find out that everyone is laughing at her for being so nakedly on the make; in five years' time she will be wanting to give it all up because she can't stand the overwork, the loneliness and the silly shoes that make her feet hurt.

As for the rest of you, it's cocooning time now. Eighties striving has been dead for a year. We move towards a kinder, gentler Britain, in which women like that will go mad, people like you will slump benignly in Majorite apathy, and people like me will seize the opportunity to trample all over you. In comfortable shoes. My feet won't hurt a bit.

30

FOLLOWING THE BREAKDOWN of talks in Geneva, everyone's attention being directed elsewhere, I have had no alternative but to annexe the United Kingdom, which has accordingly become a glorious limb of BargeCo Holdings. This will mean some significant changes in all your lives. I shall be advising you of some of your responsibilities over the coming weeks. I shall not be advising you of *all* your responsibilities because I want to be sure that I can get you whatever you do, particularly the nasty little brown-nosers who will comply with every directive. For those, there is a special Order in Chambers, made up by me just now on the toilet: *greasing up to Me is now a serious offence punishable by having to talk enthusiastically about Gazza for one hour*.

Nor shall I be advising you of your new rights and privileges. You do not have any new rights and privileges, and indeed most of your old ones have been taken away. Some of you may say, 'But what about the new right to hit, very hard, in the face, anyone found to be, claiming to be, or expressing approval of, an architect, style journalist, television presenter, politician, spokesperson, environmentalist, New Man, footballer, condom wearer or Richard Branson?' I say: you mistake yourselves. That is not a right. It is not even a privilege.

You will also notice that I said 'toilet' a few lines ago. After years of prudence and rehearsal most of you now remember to say 'loo' or even 'lavatory' but that is now illegal and punishable by six months of Barbara Cartland without the option. Similar proscriptions apply to *napkin, looking glass* and *wireless*. Furthermore, the newly constituted Snob Squad, composed almost entirely of barking mad ex-policemen who have found God, will be making spot-checks for thick corduroy trousers, Barbour jackets, fake ancestor pictures, shirts from Thomas Pink and labradors. Anyone found in possession of a telly in a Queen Anne style cabinet will be marinated, and failure to produce, on demand, an acrylic jersey, a Girobank cheque book, a pair of Bri-Nylon ski-pants in aniline blue and a photograph album containing at least one picture marked 'Brian, Steve, Jakki, ME!!!!! (Fatty!!!!!) and Lesley at Tossa del Mar' will be summarily convicted for pretensions to sophistication. The statutory punishment for this offence is being forced to eulogise Gazza for one hour at the Groucho Club while, of course, being punched in the face by Groucho members in Oliver Peoples spectacles and peculiar shoes.

Membership of the Groucho Club itself is an offence, punishable by replacement of the offender's entire wardrobe with an easi-care selection from C&A. *Nolo contendere* is your only hope, but one denied to you in the exciting Bargepole Court of Inequity where only prosecution arguments will be heard, put forward by me and adjudicated by me, too.

This is an exciting development in jurisprudence and one which will render the almost gynaecological obfuscations of our joke 'legal' system far more aerodynamic. The BCI has already sat on several occasions though the year is but young, and for your encouragement (I like to think of you waking in the middle of the night, the bed rank with sweat, screaming 'Tolpuddle! Gloophilia! Quegnosis!' until your wife (where available) punches your testicles (where available) right through your diaphragm) here are a selection of recent judgments:

IN SESSION this day of (fill in date when book-cooking time comes round, will you, honey? And a big smacker on the haunch for you too, muffin) the COURT of INEQUITY. President BARGEPOLE S J. Before the court the defendant OLINS described as an image consultant for Messrs Wolff Olins. Asked for his forename replied 'Wally.'

Bargepole S J: 'I said "name", not "occupation", damn you. You are charged with complicity in the design of British Telecom's new logo. We are not interested in how you plead nor in your arguments. You are guilty and will be forced to sit on a replica of a 1932 LNER station platform until you learn that reputation is earned by service, not bought, by purchasing with the money of discontented and cheated customers, vacuous and patronisingly infantile ideograms. Next.'

The learned BARGEPOLE S J subsequently condemned the following:

Ms Jane TCHAN, described as 'head of marketing' at the English Tourist Board, charged with describing Henry VIII as more interesting than Mozart 'because he was an international figure and has great appeal for overseas visitors'. Found guilty. Sentenced to eat regularly at bogus Tudor Banquets in the company of dry-goods salesmen from New Jersey called Wally.

Lord REES-MOGG, for living up to the absurdity of his name. Guilty. No sentence necessary in the light of Jacob Rees-Mogg, defendant's undergraduate son, who has hired a secretary to answer his correspondence at university.

Walter GIRVEN, Chief Constable of Wiltshire, for demanding further powers to make motorists blow into his little thingy, and for being called Walter in a public place. Guilty. Sentenced to make one Polo mint last 100 hours while dancing the can-can in Swindon town centre, clad only in waders and a busby.

Gianni VERSACE, for every single aspect of his lifestyle and personality. Guilty. Sentenced to live in Macclesfield as an abattoir operative.

See? And wipe that smirk off your face. You are next.

31

ELLO? HELLO? YES. Ted, I can pokka-pokka-pokka wheeeee CRUMP! hear you just fine, can you Booooooom! Thud! hear me? Uh, yes, well the situation here is very confused here in, er, here in, well in kerrrrPOW my flat, actually.

Blam! Thwock!

Yes, Yes. I think I can say that I'm here in, uh, my flat. Obviously I can't give you more precise information than that without jeopardising the operation, except that I can tell you that all of us here will be doing our best to keep you informed in this, frankly, critical period. Bang.

It's not going to be easy, obviously, and . . . hello? Hello, Ted? Ah, there you are. Seemed to me we were maybe cut off there for a second, which is something, of course, we have been expecting. I can't tell how much longer communications will hold out, although we do have an emergency backup system . . . if communications go down completely I may have to go out on to the streets here with a cheque and, uh, pay the, uh, bill at what they're already referring to here as the 'Post Office'. It has become clear that it's pretty dangerous out there on the streets at this moment. Blammmmmm! I don't know whether you caught that, Ted? Blammmmmm! See?

Uh, yes, I'm actually underneath my desk at the moment, Ted, but if I crawl across to the window – bear with me for a moment – uh, yes, the streets are fairly deserted at the present time although we have had definite warnings of a second wave coming in. However, the precise direction of that attack is uncertain, although I will be keeping you up-to-date. All I can say right now is that I am following procedure and wearing my protective NSM kit at all times, although it's . . . sorry, Ted? Oh, right, yeah. NSM, that stands for 'Nose, specs and moustache', it's a kind of rubber protective, uh, apparatus, you wear it on your head. The idea is that it confuses and hopefully, er, jams enemy identification systems, though thankfully we haven't yet had to put it to the test.

As I said, we aren't yet sure of the direction of an attack, although it has been confirmed that we are a target. What we do know is that there are considerable forces downrange, and I can confirm that American Express, the Inland Revenue and a number of other forces, including, of course, the crack Customs and Excise suicide squads, are now on a high state of alert and we are expecting incoming OHMS missives any minute. And . . .

kkkkrkkkkrkkkskssskkrkkk . . .

Uh, sorry about that, Ted, bit of static there for a moment, but I did hear what any, er, combat veteran will recognise as the sound of incoming mail, it's a sound hard to describe . . . the nearest I can get is, well, you hear this terrible sor of whistling sound – that's the delivery system – and then there's a clang as the material penetrates the building's defences, followed by a flup, and if you're wise, you eat rug the moment you hear that clang because by the time you get to the flup it's too late; as we old sweats say, 'the mail's hit the mat,' which just says it all.

And I'm getting up now, Ted, and I can tell you that the room is spinning round and round and . . . hey! this is amazing! the whole sky is a mass of colours, red and blue and violet and indigo and colours you never even thought of, all spiralling around each other in an endless whirl of crystal fire . . . oh, this is incredible, Ted, these gargantuan wings beating, beating, filling the entire sky. I can also confirm that the carpet has gone all kind of spongy, like some primeval swamp . . . yes, the carpet is definitely spongy and swampy and saturated with blood, except it's green blood, Ted, probably the green blood of the creature whose gargantuan wings you may recall I mentioned a moment ago. And at the same time my feet have turned into claws. Yes, looking down, my feet have turned into huge bronze claws which is a good thing because otherwise how could I get a grip on this spongy carpet sodden in green blood, Ted? Of course, this could be something to do with prophylactic drugs, Ted. Uh, no, I can't say for sure what the drugs actually are, but we've all been taking them for some time now, myself and Sneezy and Dopey and Bashful and . . . uh, yeah, Ted, they were provided to us by a man in sunglasses and a BMW who met us on the main drag here, known locally as Balham Hill. Yeah, I guess he was some kind of official, yeah.

Yeah, Ted, the mood of the people here is pretty good right now, there's a guy in uniform – some kind of suit – staring up at the window as I look out, but the rest of us are fine, Sneezy and Sleepy and, er, Dave, Dee, Dozy, Beaky, Mick and Titch, is it? And the naked woman handcuffed to the wardrobe, well, I say 'naked' but she's wearing black stockings and a latex bustier, that's the hell of war, huh, Ted? If the worst comes to the worst I guess we might be able to trade her for our freedom, Ted, and I want to reassure all the viewers there that if things get rough I will make sure the dwarves get out safely. We will keep filing until the last reporter is safely back home in the pub sporting his camouflage jacket and spinning bullshit about danger and nerve-gas and getting laid by lousy women.

Sorry, Ted, uh . . . Ted? Ted? Oh, hi, boss. What? Losing what grip? Well, hell, whaddya mean . . .? Insane with jealousy because nobody sent me to the Gulf? Hey, come on; you think I'm insecure? You think I've got something to prove? Well, why don't you just . . .

kkkkskskkkkkkkkkkkrsssssssssssssssssssss . . .

32

IT's A PITY about Leopold von Sacher-Masoch, because the bad woman with yellow eyes has gone barking mad again and decided to go to Israel. I am not sure that this is a good idea, the place drenched in warm fizzy drinks and chicken soup, and riddled with twitching violinists and women just like Great-Aunt Miriam, not to mention incoming missiles, but nevertheless I have decided to go with her.

My preparations are almost complete. I shot the cat this morning and have just spent two hours in the lavatory reading *The Survival Handbook* and making lists of things I will need: my special collapsible trousers, one of those intrepid camouflage jackets which make you invisible in Gloucestershire but a sitting duck in Tel Aviv, genuine desert boots and a long knife. Tomorrow I shall put all that stuff on, topped off with little red eyes glinting behind my psychotic junkie sunglasses, and go to the Tottenham Court Road to intimidate my money out of the woman I did the television advertisement for, then it's back home, into the sober grey suit, and heigh-ho for the open road, the wide blue yonder, the bombs, the guns and the gas.

I don't know why I am doing this. Every time I set foot west of the forty-degree meridian I end up in prison or in hospital, and occasionally both. What's more, it's a bad time to leave. A fortune-teller made eyes at me in a basement the other day and I have never had a go on a fortune-teller before. It might be terrible: 'I knew you were going to do that . . .' But I have a few tricks up my sleeve and no amount of astrology, necromancy or clairvoyance could predict my *tour de force*, the one with the Velcro, the pomegranate and the Bovril. Looking on the bright side, what is it all anyway but a squeal, a wriggle and a lot of inconvenience: shouting, recriminations, wandering around in the middle of the night looking for Kleenex, Swarfega, chicken livers and brake fluid? I can do without that sort of stuff and so can you, if you are honest with yourself.

On the other hand, I can probably do without being blown up as well. They say that if it's got your name on it, there's nothing you can do, but what about the ones marked *To Whom It May Concern*? They also say you never hear the one that gets you, but that's rubbish, too. You hear it perfectly clearly but then it gets you, so you can't leap around sniggering and making V-signs, shouting: 'Heard it! *Heard* it! Nah nah-ni nah nah!'

My biggest misgiving, however, is gas. The bad yellow-eyed woman is okay *vis-à-vis* gas, so she says. 'No problem *vis-à-vis* gas,' she said. 'Not for me. I have an entree with the BBC. They do gas masks. Easy peasy. You get them from International Relations.' Which goes to show what the BBC thinks about world harmony and the *Pax Americana*.

'What about me?' I whined, in my rugged, swashbuckling way. 'Tough,' she said. 'You'll have to make do with a wet towel and some baking soda. But you'll have to buy your own. International Relations don't do towels and baking soda, and even if they did you couldn't have any because you're not accredited. I don't know why you're coming, anyway. I was looking forward to missing you.'

Were it not for Leopold von Sacher-Masoch, there would be no problem. I could just potter down to Zeitgeist, the aptly named fetishists' emporium in Soho, and buy more gas masks than you could shake a rubber cat-o'-nine-tails at. The trouble is, it appears to be L v S M's anniversary (though I don't quite see which one: it's probably just an excuse), and all over Britain, fetishists have been winkling out their old gas masks for the gala knees-up. 'What do you think, dear?' they have been hooting, in a muffled sort of way behind the yellowing mica peepholes. 'Ooh, no,' say their spouses, just like that beastly woman in the Yellow Pages panama hat advertisement: 'No, you can't go out like that, you'd better get a new one, and while you're at it you'd better give your rubber leggings a rubover with Mister Sheen.'

It's the only explanation. Two weeks ago you could have bought enough gas masks to equip a whole reef-knot of perverts. There was even a choice of colour, the traditional black, or a kind of wimpy grey like those shoes worn by the sort of people who buy little air-fresheners to fit inside the bog roll. But now you can't get any. My only hope is my fetishist friend in Paris, but I think there may be problems there, too, and nothing to do with L v S M, either, oh no, *she* doesn't need an excuse, it's straight home from work and into the gas mask and the latex straitjacket for a cosy evening on the rack. I suppose I could always chain her to the ironing board and simply *steal* the damned thing, but one is, after all, a clean-living, right-thinking sort of a chap and such jiggery (pokery doesn't come into it) will not do.

So there we are. When the gas bombs start landing all over Europe, the only ones to survive will be the fetishists and the BBC folk, snug in their little outfits. Presently they will emerge, blinking, into the light, smiling shyly at each other, ready to begin the whole dismal process all over again. In the meantime, I shall simply have to struggle with bicarbonate of soda and a wet towel, and if the result is anything like the mango and Roquefort soufflé I made the other day it will take more than a spoonful of Veno's and a quarter of sensemila to put me right. And if you think *that's* in bad taste, what about the flouncing, irascible uniform queens who started all this? Bunch of fairies, that's what I say. What do *you* say?

33

JERUSALEM. *EAST* JERUSALEM, to be precise. One must be. That is what we are like, we foreign correspondents, out here in the War Zone. You can tell I am a foreign correspondent. Room looks like a Scud has hit it, the result of carefully stage-managed distressing and casting-about of props. Half-gallon of Famous Grouse on the ash-stained desk (I always carry a small bag of ash, otherwise I would have to spend hours smoking cigarettes). Trusty brass Zippo, mirror sunglasses, Swiss army knife, canisters of film, battered black Leica (bought last Thursday but battered by me on the flight over). Why is the film not in the Leica? Because I do not know how to do that. But so what? The Leica is not to take pictures with, it is to hang round my neck when I go down to the Cellar Bar to talk to other foreign correspondents, here in the War Zone, which I will do after I have stopped typing this.

I am wearing only underpants.

This is what we foreign correspondents, here in the War Zone, do. It is germane, stylish, epigrammatic, *essential*.

It is good, this: good for me, but most of all good for you. Do you know how lucky you are, you bastards? Do you know what we do for you, here in the War Zone? We go to the restaurant. We take our lives in our hands. Outside the restaurant a notice, decorated with two round bombs like cartoon anarchists carry, says:

'Guests MUST bring their gas masks into the restaurant with them. In a real emergency there is not time to fetch them from rooms.

'There is no guarantee that no rockets will land in Jerusalem.'

See? And we do not only take those risks. Sometimes we go out to restaurants, walking through the streets of

East Jerusalem as though they were perhaps the safest places in the world, constantly patrolled by police and the military, nobody about, no street crime, safer than St James's Street at noon. So what if that is indeed how it is? Even were it otherwise, we would be out there, taking risks to bring you the truth, sticking together because nobody else will talk to us because we have Leicas hung round our necks, and notebooks sticking out, and special War Zone waistcoats with 27 pockets and a diagram to tell you which pocket everything is in, except one can never be sure which pocket the diagram is in.

So we talk to each other, and compare waistcoats, and watch CNN in our rooms here in the War Zone, its manic posturings and facile lamentations drifting out past the Anglican Cathedral and the Rockefeller Museum, past Herod's gate and along the Via Dolorosa, a nod at the Western Wall and then growing fainter, past the dome of the Rock where Christians sleep and dream of slaughtering other Christians who are heretical about the fingernails of St Chrysostom or who once complained about the food at the Council of Nicea . . . and eventually coming to rest in Gethsemane.

You might think the memory or image of Reb Yeshua, who nearly two thousand years ago wandered Gethsemane, not god-like at all but a hunched, wild-eyed knot of visceral terror, would not be forgotten, but here in the *Jerusalem Post*, Rabbi Menachem Scheerson explains that the Mashiach Ben-Yosef, the first, preparatory Messiah, is due to arrive around Pesach. 'Don't bother taking your Megilla,' he is said to have told a Jewish American soldier on his way to the Gulf. The Megilla is the scroll of the book of Esther, traditionally read aloud on Purim, this Thursday. A good feast, Purim, and another of its traditions is the wearing of masks. This tradition will be comprehensively observed, I think, this year, unless Rantal Ltd of 13 Yordei Hasira have their way. 'Why take a risk? No need for gas masks. In a shelter fitted with our system, you are protected from chemical, biological and atomic attack.' But are you protected against the new Mashiach?

But we foreign correspondents need not concern ourselves with such things. It is not our business to give a damn, as I have already had to explain at knifepoint to the bad yellow-eyed woman who within 24 hours had gone barking mad, crying out her tiny eyes (reddened with severe withdrawal, since I have cut off her whisky supply, reserving it for my personal use) about the plight of the Palestinians.

'Pftui!' I said – *you* try it, it feels Gallic and good – 'Pftui, we foreign correspondents don't give a stuff about the Palestinians, we identify the winning side and stick with it, those buggers are landless, they are locked up in their houses, they get shot, their crops are rotting in the orange groves, they are, in short, *losers*. Weep not for them, but be like me: call them "terrorists" and spit on the name of Arafat.'

And now the yellow-eyed woman wants to go to Gaza in the occupied territories. Fool. Everyone knows they are the *administered* territories, and there's nothing to see anyway. If there were, it would be on CNN. No need to stir. Even the French foreign correspondents – *real* hot-shots with Mitsubishi Shogun 4WDs, and *suede* photojournalist waistcoats with twice the usual number of pockets, and *two Leicas each* – even they haven't said anything about the terrorists.

A monoglot Russian émigré is staging Gilbert & Sullivan. Down in the bar the American aid workers are at each other's throats. A Belgian journalist has been ostracised for cheating. Camel filter are $2 a packet. These are taxing times, tough but thrilling. You get big balls in the War Zone. Would I lie?

34

A WARM ROCK in Qumran is a fine place to sit on the last day of the war, with a bottle of oily, sweet Sabra, looking across the Dead Sea towards Jordan while the bad yellow-eyed woman potters aimlessly among the stones. The wind boistering down from Galilee is as damp and relentless as a dog's tongue but my keffiyeh protects me from this wet and gritty saltiness.

A black-patterned keffiyeh signifies Palestinian affiliations, red, Jordanian: mine is black-and-red, so I should be safe from myopic Jordanians paddling across Ham Ha-Melah and from resentful Palestinians perched atop the Midbar Yehuda mountains to my back. If a carload of Israelis should come down the road, though, I am probably buggered: these people are all military reservists, armed to the teeth, and here I sit, defiling the sacred stones – sacred to the Jews, that is; to a *faux*-Arab like me, they are mere ammunition.

But never mind. The Israelis will not come: they are all staying at home for the time being, and the shores of the Dead Sea are deserted, save from the occasional military patrol and the yellow-eyed woman, who is too small to show on radar.

Two millennia ago, the Essenes lived here, sequestered from the Jewish establishment, which they found too liberal. It might have been easier for them just to lighten up a bit, but they chose this arid desolation between the rocks and a wet place, and in its rich, heavy air, a thousand feet below sea level, they thrived after their fashion.

They passed their time studying Torah and writing the Dead Sea Scrolls. They didn't know that they were the Dead Sea Scrolls, of course – that would take another two thousand years – but they wrote them anyway, and rolled them up, and hid them in caves. I have a certain sympathy with the Essenes.

The other thing they did was fight. Isolated as they were, there was nevertheless one other community of zealots at Massada. They lived in an impregnable hilltop fort some thirty miles south along the shore, and every now and then they would come down to fight the Essenes. When the Romans turned up, the Essenes and the zealots fought the Romans too, although they never stopped fighting each other.

Some reports say that the Massada zealots wiped out the Qumran Essenes, and other reports say that the Romans wiped out both of them, and yet other reports say that the Romans were just about to wipe out the zealots when the zealots pre-empted them by committing mass suicide. Whatever happened, the zealots and the Essenes were comprehensively shafted, and now both Massada and Qumran are holy places, commemorating something-or-other about the zealots and the Essenes which I can't quite put my finger on.

I think it's probably their pig-headed stupidity, their determined separatism, their religious zeal and their complete inability to join cause in the face of a common enemy.

We tend to think of evolution and progress as being almost the same thing, but half-an-hour's brainwork and Sabra on the Qumran stones makes it clear that that's nonsense. On the one hand you have evolution, the means by which one species turns into another by adapting to its environment; and on the other hand you have progress, whereby a given species learns a thing or two about dealing with the environment into which it has evolved, and so improves its quality of life. Evolution is a fact of life throughout the Earth, but progress seems to be a regional speciality. And the Middle East is not one of those regions.

It's hard to know how to deal with this. The bad yellow-eyed woman's response is 'Poor old Middle East', which seems to me about the strength of it. US Secretary of State Baker is due in Jerusalem any day now to persuade the Israelis not to boycott international peace talks. The Israelis are against peace talks because they don't want to get yet another earful about the Palestinians. The Palestinians are sort of against international peace talks because they haven't yet had time to indulge in the traditional outburst of post-war stone-throwing, let alone time to decide whether they want to be represented by (a) Saddam Hussein (b) Yasser Arafat (c) the Hamas/Jihad Islam alliance or (d) Jordan. On the other hand they support the idea of a peace conference (a) because Israel doesn't and (b) because they particularly enjoy the sight of Mr Shamir revealing yet again that he is barking mad, frothing like a throttled hyrax (a small desert lynx which will wait for days until a lone car approaches before trying to cross the highway).

The only 'solution' to the Middle East that I can see is that there isn't a solution, and the only thing that the world can do is gather round and say 'Poor old Middle East', before paying everyone their coalition disbursements so that they can all rush off to Moscow and re-arm themselves to the teeth.

All this is of course incomprehensible to the West, except for those of us blessed with the blood of old Ireland coursing in our veins. It's all there: the tribal loyalties, the obsession with politics, the unwillingness to do anything constructive, the hypnotic urge to get together and sing th'ould songs, the gratifying combination of swaggering and whining, the secret societies, the colours, the crack and the rumpus.

You bleeding hearts can go to Hell. This is a fine place, like Ireland with the sunshine, and I may just stay here for good, d'ye hear me?

35

WHAT FUN IT IS to be back in the liberal humanist West. Willies, willies all the way, or so it seems at the first, bleary glance, stumbling off the El Al Jumbo into the beastliness of Heathrow.

They took one last shot at me on board. Word had obviously been sent from the black-eyed, big-breasted security control woman at Ben Gurion airport. As a parting '*bon voyage*' from the Holy Land, she took my luggage to pieces and demanded to see copies of everything I had written while in Israel. Why had I come? Where had I been? Had I made any friends?

I don't know what the penalty is for making friends in Israel. Probably you get put under a dawn-to-dusk curfew, and if you make any more friends after that, they knock down your house and fill in your artesian well. So I played safe. 'Friends?' I said. '*Friends*? Good Lord, no. Had enough of that in 'Nam. Yo.'

Ground security was not amused. It pottered off, swinging its hips and pouting, and sent over another one, smaller, wirier, athletic-looking, the sort who could wrestle a man to the bed and shout 'Yes! Yes! Give it to me, big boy!' without laughing. This one then asked me exactly the same questions all over again and then the original one came back, and they *both* asked me the same questions, all over again, again.

The bit which particularly worried them was the bad yellow-eyed woman. Why was she remaining in Israel when I was returning? Why? What did I mean, I had to get back? Why did I have to get back? *Why*? Somebody had *told* me to get back, hadn't they? Someone had come up to me in the airport and told me I had to get back, was that not the case? All right, then, so someone had come up to me the night before and told me I had to get back, hadn't they? And they had given me something to take back too, hadn't they, something wrapped in oiled paper, smelling faintly of almonds with two batteries sticking out of the side? Hadn't they? *Hadn't they?*

Ah. So nobody had come up to me, was that what I was saying? Nobody at all. Not even a friend . . .

Well sucks to that old trap. I could see it a mile off. 'So you *did* make a friend, then, you smirking, pork-gobbling, milk-and-blood heathen imperialist! Komm mit uns!' With the sort of delicate, high speed intellectual swerve which betrays years of dealing with the American Express debt collection department, I pointed out that the only 'friend' I had talked to about returning to England was the bad yellow-eyed woman. Good grief, I hadn't even mentioned my departure to the hotel; I had simply loaded my luggage into the hired car before dawn, gone in to breakfast, heaped my plate with pork sausages and wandered blearily off like a man going for a matutinal widdle. Why, the hotel probably didn't even know I had gone.

At this, ground security pricked up. So if the bad yellow-eyed woman was my only friend, how come I was going and she was staying behind? Was I going to explain that or was I not?

'Fine,' I said. Time was ticking away and I could hear the pilot revving up at the starting gate. 'I'll tell you the truth. We have been confined to small rooms and small cars for over a month. We have been interrogated, stoned, manipulated and traduced. We have been fed propaganda and lies by everyone, including, inexplicably, a Syrian currant-trader with a rubber foot who I suspect came illicitly over the Golan heights on a tea-tray specifically to lie to us. We have not been out of each other's eyesight for a thousand hours, yet there has not been a cross word between us. But she has now gone completely off her oats, and so I'm going to London for a bit of a poke, otherwise I turn crabby and get black spots in front of my eyes.

Unless . . . what are either of you ladies doing this evening?'

Zionism and the Jewish Homeland have between them erased much of the *shtetl* mentality, yet, curiously, they still speak Yiddish at times of stress. '*Pischer*,' they murmured to each other in a finely graded crescendo of graduated calumny. '*Schmegeggie*.' '*Schlemiel*.' '*Pascudnik*.' '*Schvantz*.' '*Schmuck*.' '*Potz*.' Then they waved me through, ordered me to have a nice flight, and turned to a middle-aged man who looked as though he had a guilty secret; perhaps he had once bought a bag of dates from a Wicked Palestinian in Nablus market . . .

The message was sent ahead, though, and when they came around with the duty-free, somewhere over Yugoslavia, they were ready for me. I only realised when I got to Heathrow and tried to buy a newspaper that they had given me all my change in old, illegal shillings. 'Give them to the *goyische potz*,' the service message had gone out. 'That bastard tried to proposition two of our Brave Israeli Girls.'

But eventually I got my newspaper. I thought the Middle East was insane, but this is worse. Men are living in fear of their wives, being beaten with pots and pans, sent to the shed and convicted of rape when they try to make it up. A middle-aged impotent homosexual has caught Aids from beating up fruits. And a soldier who went to hospital for a skin graft woke up to find they had chopped his willy off. He's now suing them for damages. How odd; how short-sighted. The doctors have done him a favour. If somebody had chopped my willy off years ago my life would now be very different. I wouldn't be bankrupt. I wouldn't be myopic. I wouldn't have had a crack at ground security and I certainly wouldn't have two pockets-full of useless shillings weighing down my jeans (uncomfortably snug, but women find them attractive, you see).

36

WELL I HAD to tell her, I said, look, lovey, I'm sure he *adores* you but don't you think it's a little odd that he should go on about it, I mean, what sort of man rings up from the airport and tells you he doesn't *want* to go on a stag party to Amsterdam with a bunch of professional people, you know, a nice bunch of people, accountants, barristers, probably a dentist or two, they are all doing well, I bet you half of them have got, oh, I don't know, Golf GTi convertibles, pension plans, I expect they've got American Express Gold Cards, half of them, I mean, you know, I had to tell her.

Doesn't *want* to go? I said. Look, lovey, I said, of *course* he wants to go, looking forward to it, I expect, probably been waking up with a stiffy in anticipation for weeks, nobody goes to Amsterdam for the Rijksmuseum, what they go for is sex, there are things going on there that would make your eyes bubble, none of your Two In A Bed Sex Romps for the Dutch, not the *Dutch*, the *Dutch* are too busy being liberals and doing town planning and stopping the politicians getting above themselves, no, it's for the tourists.

Oh no, I said, no, you've got it *completely* wrong, I said, it's *exactly* people like that who go to brothels, that's who brothels are for, little Englishmen who know the rules, stick with their own sort, the sort who have something subtly but horribly wrong with their Y-Fronts. Fornication? But 'twas in another country, and besides the wench was black.

I know *he's* not like that, I said, but they're *all* like that, it's not the excitement of surfing earnestly, teeth gritted, on the further shores of bizarre sex, that's for Germans, they screw like they bank, with fierce dedication and a lot of accessories, no, dear, I said, they'll get queasily drunk on lager and then hoof it around the old city walls burping and looking shiftily at each other, not actually *going* nudge nudge wink wink follow my meaning get my drift, eh?, *eh*?, PHWOOOOR!!!!, but certainly *thinking* it, until one of them says, 'Let's go in here, we don't have to do anything but you can't go to Amsterdam on a stag night without actually, you know, and anyway, old Charlie' (or Hugo or Marco or some equally objectionable hot-socks-and-cold-pizza name) 'won't get another chance after the knot's tied hah hah hah,' and that's that, I said.

Anyway a week later she's back, out it comes, just as I said, well, I said, I told you, didn't I, I *told* you, oh, I know how you must feel, *yes*, but that's men all over, isn't it? So, I said, let me give you all the details, look, lovey, I might as well have been there myself, heard it a million times, he comes home all damp and pasty-looking and says there's something he's got to tell you, they're transparent, it's pathetic really . . . and he says he didn't want to go inside, not really, but, well, you know, and so he goes off with this one girl, 30 quid it costs him for a hand job but he didn't do anything, not actually *do* anything, couldn't, you know, couldn't er, er crack a fat, get a stiffy hwark hwark probly too much lager akshly, God how *awful* but apsley couldm'pt do a thing, but it's all right anyway because she made him wear a you know, *thingy*.

Well of course that's *precisely* what happened according to him, so I said to her, I said, look, never mind the rest of it, how come she made him wear a, you know, thing, when he couldn't, you know, too much lager and so on? And she says: ah.

So I said to her, look, that may be exactly what did happen or alternatively he may have leapt in joyfully shouting 'This one's for the Sudetenland, you squareheaded pipesucking collaborators,' but that doesn't matter, that's not the point, I said. The point, I said, the point is that he's guilty of bad taste and lack of style, I said. I mean, look, I said, believe me, you are a pocket Venus, everything just as it should be, if you don't believe me slip out of your things, pass me that bottle of almond oil and those handcuffs and I'll *show* you, lovey, I said, but don't expect to get out of here in under four hours.

So she cheered up a bit and I said, look, I said, the least he could have done was take you along, never mind the nice young professional men, the two of you could have gone off to Club Doma in the Hague, 107 Alsterstraat, latex, leather, public S&M, everything you could want, he doesn't know how to appreciate you, I said, that's where I'm going to take that Alice, you know, the gorgeous one, the one with the panther tattoo and the *Traumbusen*, the one who said she'd do anything if I just mentioned her name, I don't think she knows what she's let herself in for, I said, but it won't be me going off to Amsterdam and coming back with a limp story like *that*, I said.

And anyway what sort of man claims impotence in order to evade a woman's wrath? Where's his *cojones*, I said, but she said, 'I don't know what you're talking about, I think he's sweet, you're just trying to get me into bed, he's asked me to marry him and I said I'd think about it.'

Bed, I said, *bed*, I can think of nothing nicer but I'm a man of honour and anyway the bad yellow-eyed woman would rip my throat out although she need never know, and I certainly won't tell her about Alice with the panther tattoo. I'm out of action at the moment, my joints have locked up, the doctor says it's equine gonorrhoea. I don't remember having it off with a horse but I suppose it was probably last Thursday. Thursdays are always tricky, and she said, 'You are all the same,' and I said, suit yourself, isn't that precisely what I've been trying to tell you?

Honestly. Some people.

37

GREEN MIST ON the windless fields, and the woodsmoke rising to hang above the peaceful village. Honey-coloured girls, like dreams or goldfish, smile sweetly and slip out of their things. Old men croak, as old men should. But wait: here comes an American, crunching through the undergrowth in his Timberland Weathergear. He is immortal, free, the Heir of Ages; he has a Rolex GMT-Master II, a Nikon F4 and an American Express card, and has been brought up on neon-toothed TV game shows. Everything is going to be all right now that the US trade embargo is being lifted. He is bringing the joys of Civilisation to Vietnam.

In anticipation, the Thai hookers are tripping across the Mekong and taking the Ho Chi Minh Trail. They are calling it 'Saigon' again, and the paid fellatrices will be followed by others, more ignoble and worse value for money: McDonald's, Burger King and AmEx, paunchy wet-lipped, clammy-templed bleeding hearts in Hugo Boss lightweight suits, microchip entrepreneurs, gasoline touts, car dealers and HVAC vendors, feminist educationalists with cystitis and executives with chlamydia and grumpy wives.

Soon the Vietnamese will be declared officially Black, and the Reverend (suggesting someone reveres him, but who?) Al Sharpton will be along with his Michigan trailer-housewife hair-do and his pimp medallion to tell them that they are downtrodden. Because they are downtrodden they will wonder who the hell the Reverend Al Sharpton is, and who it is, precisely, that reveres him; and they will wonder why his bodyguards wear mirror-lens RayBans indoors.

Soon, too, the British will be able to contribute. We could send Denis Tunnicliffe, the managing director of London Underground, to let them have a look at his pouchy, ruined 'face'. We could even, if they are very good and eat their Big Macs without throwing up, send them Westminster Council's environmental health officers, too: the ones who have threatened to confiscate Mr Antoin O Dochartaigh's bagpipes if he continues to play them without a licence, and, at the same time, told him that he can't have a licence anyway. If that is the state of their minds, can you imagine the state of their groins?

All this will be wonderful for the Vietnamese. Don't you see? The Americans will teach them that you don't have to think before you swagger, provided you are able to buy things you neither need nor want at any hour of the day or night without having to pay until later.

They will also teach them cultural relativism. It is the foolish pride of the Vietnamese that got them into trouble in the first place: now they will learn that they are no better nor worse than anyone else, that the God of Israel is no greater than a turnip-ghost or a mummy on a stick, that !Xhosa is as eloquent as Shakespeare and Shakespeare no better than MC Hammer, that Europe, far from being the steward of civilisation for a millennium and more, is the home of Dead White European Males who are irrelevant, illiberal, sexist and élitist, that, in short, nothing is better than anything providing it is all-American.

They will learn to love the smell of bagels in the morning.

And we British will act as the counterpoise. Under the tutelage of the men from Westminster Council, we will teach them how to ban things. This is a time for pride. I do not want to hear about our failures-to-ban. You may say that we have not banned Paul Raymond or the Virgin Megastore or the £2 hot dog made of fish, breadcrumbs and rat nostrils, or multiple sequential road-digging, or the public display of dark hairy bum-clefts, or trainers and anoraks, or taxi drivers who want you to guess how much their brother takes home in a week, go on, how much, or urine-sodden tube stations, or Sony Walkmen, or adolescent clubbers in baseball hats, or the chef making an appearance in the dining-room, or fat couples from Kingston in matching Nike tracksuits with the trouser-creases sewn in, or executives in grey shoes in Madame Jo-Jo, or Nigel Kennedy, or late-night supermarkets.

But think what we *have* banned. Street musicians, unlicensed theatrical performances, blue movies, drinking in the street, drinking after hours, drinking on Sundays, staying out late unless you can afford a taxi, various kinds of jam, various kinds of sausage, eating in the open air, playing on the grass, shooting bats, keeping tortoises, gassing badgers, playing the bagpipes, singing the old songs, playing cards, having a bet, adopting a different-coloured child, parking the car, telling Irish jokes, eating hedgehog crisps, feeding the animals, picking the flowers, knowing the facts.

This is something to be proud of, and something the Vietnamese will welcome. Their embracing of communism shows their willingness to endure hardships and discomfort for the sake of an ideology. Now we can take them a step further on the Drizzling Path: the enduring of hardship and discomfort for its own sake.

Soon they will stop enjoying food, sex or the sunshine. Presently, if they play their cards right, they will come up with their own television game shows, convenience foods and tabloid newspapers. And – who knows – if they are *very* good, and absorb the essentials of British and American culture, they may manage to produce, simultaneously, their own indigenous Bernard Manning and their own indigenous Bret Easton Ellis. And wouldn't *that* be lovely?

38

IT MUST BE SPRING. Everyone is going mad again. They ring me up and complain about their damned relationships. Whinge, whinge, whinge. 'He won't tie me up.' 'He wants to tie me up.' 'She despises me.' 'He said he couldn't see me because he was working, but I found out he was off seeing that horrid friend of his.' 'He wouldn't even tell his wife he was having a drink with me. He's ashamed of me because I'm gay but I've got feelings like anyone else. More so, in fact.' 'Yes, I know I left her but now I want her back again.'

Phooey to that. As far as I am concerned, it's all sorted out. One-in-a-bed sex romps pass the time pleasantly enough, the bad yellow-eyed woman is usually lurking around somewhere eating Whiskas from the tin with her feet, and the wren-boned features editress has said I can demolish her lean-to bathroom and six potting sheds. Nuts to women problems.

I seem to be the only one, though. I expect it is to do with my insouciance, my intellect, my massive potency and my Harland & Wolff bridgework, but from my lofty invulnerability I survey the rest of you and I feel pity. Pity.

So I have been trying to think of something which may help. There's this American woman, of course, the professor of linguistics, who says that men talk a different language from women and if we could only understand each other it would all be fine. The theory is that everything men say is about preserving their own status, while everything women say is about bonding. I'm not sure that it's entirely true, given the amount of time we spend on theology, physics, gossip and smut, but there may be something to it. The only trouble is that, as far as I can see, 'learning to understand each other' seems to translate as 'men learning to talk like women', and I would hesitate to recommend a course of action which would lead to millions of pudgy re-insurance consultants in Harrods suits nattering away like a pack of big girls' blouses.

But there is another way. Go along to The Mall Gallery and stick your beak into the Royal Society of Portrait Painters centenary exhibition. There, hanging among the fatties and bimbos, is an image for our times. It is a picture of Mrs Andrew Baylis, painted by someone called Carlos Sancha, and it will take the fur off your tongue just to see it. Who Andrew Baylis is, or was, I do not know. The name has not appeared in any national newspaper for the past seven years. And nothing is revealed by the painting of Mrs Andrew Baylis. She sits in front of a horrid screen on a horrid sofa in a horrid room next to some horrid flowers, wearing the sort of multi-petticoated sticky-out frock that people's wives wear to Home Counties parties where there's someone called Basil, and someone called Derek, and an undertow of bridge rolls and Jaguar upholstery and gin.

The picture could have been painted yesterday or in 1953. And that is the secret. Here, frozen for ever in Carlos Sancha's brush-strokes, is permanence. Here is stability. Here is an end to our endless misunderstandings, our yearning, the bad midnight stuff, the raids on the inarticulate, the raids on the fridge, the sad sex, the skirmishes, the nasty streets and the bimbo gristle in cheap flats. Here is the way forward. The portrait of Mrs Andrew Baylis is an image of mute possession, of life as a process of acquisition in which everything must be reduced to the status of property and then bought and kept and boasted about. Just as the couple in Jan van Eyck's 'The Arnolfini Marriage' have become icons, so, too, Mrs Andrew Baylis has become public property, and her own identity and that of her husband cease to matter.

What is of consequence is what the painting offers us: an image of a life where it is All Sorted Out. Of the real Andrew Baylis we know nothing. But, purely as an icon, the picture evokes a peculiarly British dream. It is a dream of power and possession, of things one doesn't talk about and things one doesn't do. Of a life carefully designed to exclude the uncontrollable, to minimise the unexpected, to prevent questions being raised.

Of the boardroom dinner, the house in Eaton Terrace, the trip to Glyndebourne. Of charity balls, overprinted Christmas cards, Persian cats, hair by Michaeljohn. The bedroom is frilly and the drawing room is chintz, but there is Regency stripe in the dining room. The talk is about shares and politics. There is no communication, for none (except that which can be contained on a cheque) is needed.

Of life that leads to a seat in the Lords. It is an English life. And hundreds upon thousands of such English lives, led like that, have brought us to today: to the end of Rolls-Royce at Mulliner Park Ward. To an Englishwoman in space, but no English money. (Because how can we be sure?) To the despicable advertisements of the NatWest Bank. To compulsory seat belts in taxis. To the abominable Sundayishness of English life, dull and ponderous timidity while the dispossessed whirl jerkily around the periphery on their puffy Nike shoes, chanting the sentiments of rap rather than take the risk of thinking.

And over it all, the icon of Mrs Andrew Baylis, hovering like the Black Madonna of Czestochowa, for us to gaze at, not with fear or awe, or yearning, or hope or piety, but with the spiritual equivalent of the smell of too much carpet: above all, with nothing which could ruffle the glassy surface of our own terminal mediocrity.

Spring. Ah, spring.

39

M Y DOMAINS ARE extensive and little normally dis-
turbs the silence save the drip of brackish water or
the touching screams of the small amphibians which
my man, Kington, selects as my partners for the night. We are
well-supplied with green friends, so loneliness is not a problem
and I am normally content to pass my time without human
company. In the dry season, when the amphibians shrivel and
nature is harsh, I used to fret but now all I have to do is go to
the Whitley Bridge garage, near Pontefract, where there is a
round-the-clock maggot machine.

People who argue against technology will surely be converted by this marvellous example of man's ingenuity. No
more hanging around outside some horrid back-street shop
in the wind-whipped dawn, waiting for the proprietor to rise
from his enseaméd bed and start dishing up the maggots. One
simply leaps into the helicopter, checks one's trousers for the
necessary loose change and heads for Whitley Bridge.

The journey is quick and the time passes easily in deciding
which maggots to have. There are red ones, at £1.20 the tin;
bronze ones, at £1.20 the tin; or fluorescent pink, at £1.20
the tin. For purists, there are white maggots, at £1.20 the
tin, and for the indecisive, £1.20 will buy a tin of mixed
maggots.

The maggot machine, modestly, says 'Fishing Bait' and
'Bag it with Mag-It'. But the Mag-It people underestimate
their service, which can eliminate many of life's problems: night starvation, bedtime loneliness, designing women,
croaking in the dark.

Hungry? Never mind trudging in the rain to the 7-Eleven
for a delicious, hand-microwaved, EEC-approved Cornish-
type pasty; simply ring the bell and in comes Kington,
immaculately dressed, his Japanese transistor (as always)

pressed to his ear, with a tin of best bronze ready-opened on a Benares brassware tray. Lonely in the dark? A tin of fluorescent pinks emptied into a Marigold washing-up glove will solace even the longest nights, easily visible even by the thin, weedy glow from the ancestral Wombles nite-lite. Women in print frocks hanging around and talking wistfully about babies? A tin of pallid, moist whites, like little executives, scattered around the legs of her chair, or around the legs of her self, or perhaps even placed in the toes of her Kurt Geiger pumps as she sleeps the sleep of the smug, will have her running from the premises yelping 'Ugh! Ugh! I have never seen anything so disgusting in my life!' And, of course, a tinful of plump reds, stored in a warm room and allowed to hatch, will keep at bay the croaking of rejected amphibia as they honk and blart for alimony, affection and food.

But, of course, you won't take advantage of the Mag-It, will you? Oh, there may be some feeble-minded characters who, having never even thought of maggots before, will, now that they are available, be creeping out of bed at three in the morning, pulling their trousers over their winceyette pyjamas, and pedalling off to Pontefract in the sleet. There, they will hang around importuning passers-by for change until they have enough for a fix of maggots; and, having them, will not know what to do with them. (This is the English way: disproportionate desire followed at once by incomprehension and neglect. That is why we like sheds so much. We need somewhere to keep all the things that we desperately wanted until we got them.)

The rest of you will take comfort from knowing that the Mag-It is there but will you go to Whitley Bridge? Will you shell out a measly £1.20? Will you give gaily wrapped tins of maggots to your friends for Christmas? Will you buggery. What you will do is sit there, maggotless, vaguely aware of how maggots might alter your life but doing nothing about it, until one day some smirking cheat from the National Westminster Bank, making sure that people don't make the same mistakes his old man did, forecloses on the Mag-It man and the Mag-It of Whitley Bridge is taken away.

Then you will raise merry hell, of course. You will write to your MP. You will sit on the lavatory nodding in petulant agreement at Gavin Stamp's diatribe in the *Spectator*. You will talk about it at dinner parties with Jenny, Wobbler, Lucinda and old Dogbreath who's riding out the recession rather well.

How do I know? Because you've done it before. You believed all the lies the banks told you in the Eighties, and now you are moaning about the recession. You bought your electricity shares and your water shares and now you moan about the bills. You voted for Mrs Thatcher and now you moan that you are having to remove your own gangrenous leg on the kitchen table. You paid through the snout for champagne and bresaola, and now you moan that the restaurants can't survive now you're skint. You complained about the old telephone boxes which you couldn't get into and then couldn't get out again, suffocating in the stench of urine, and then complained when Telecom replaced them. You fell for all that Peter Mayle bullshit and now moan that Provence is being spoiled.

The silence of my domains has been disturbed this week by people telephoning me to ask foolish questions about the 150th anniversary of this organ. 'Will it survive?' they ask; 'What is wrong with it?' and 'Do you hate the editor?' Dolts. Of course I hate the editor. Every columnist hates his editor. It is part of the contract. As for the other questions, why do they immediately make me think of the likely fate of the wonderful Mag-It?

40

THE SLOTH, IN infancy, is, as sloths go, lively. But it is also inept; so inept that it frequently grasps its own limbs, mistaking them for tree-branches. It then crashes through the foliage and hits the deck (or 'exhibits deck-hitting behaviour,' as a zoologist would say, as if the sloth were somehow doing it for our benefit, as a kind of sideshow).

If you are in the right place at the right time you can witness it all: a yelp, a crashing of vegetation, and a thud, and then an infant sloth lying there, dazed but still clinging on, wondering what went wrong.

Its puzzlement is reasonable. After all, it did what sloths are meant to do: took a firm hold and maintained its grip. All should be well; but all is not well.

Presently, the infant sloth learns an important lesson. It is a good lesson. It is a lesson which bears fruit. But it is the wrong lesson. For the lesson that the infant sloth learns is sloth. 'Concerning limbs,' it reasons, 'find a reliable one and stick with it. All this fancy branch-to-branch stuff is unproductive and dangerous to boot.'

This is fine as far as it goes, which is nowhere. True, the sloth remains satisfactorily aloft, but its life lacks enterprise. It is not the sort of life of which a marketing man would approve. Doing public relations for a sloth would be an uphill struggle.

There is a profound lesson here for all of us. The sloth is a metaphor for something so deeply rooted and significant in our natures that I simply have no idea what it is. And I can't say I really give a damn. I don't even care if it's all rubbish about the sloth. I didn't go and check. I didn't even read about it myself. Someone told me that he'd read it somewhere and that'll have to do. No doubt, at the end of the trail, there's a hot man in a wet jungle looking at a sloth, but that man is not I, nor, indeed, will it ever be.

This cast of mind unfits me for many things. Were I a detective, Hercule Poirot need not fear. I would get as far as assembling the house-party in the library, but then would simply send in the butler to tell them that I neither knew who did it, nor cared. Had God called me to be a polevaulter, I would be found leaning on my pole, reasoning that if one wanted suddenly to lie down in some sand, there was no need whatsoever to jump over a bar to do it. Similarly, I would have been a rotten surgeon. Why cut someone open only to sew them up again? A complete waste of time, if you ask me: time which could far more valuably be spent gawping.

Yet there has never been a time when gawping has been less fashionable. We used to be good at it, we British. We founded a whole Empire on gawping. The rest of the world only noticed the preparatory stage, the part where we would grow moustaches, buy white duck clothes, and push off to subdue the natives somewhere. What they didn't realise was that, once we had subdued them, we sat on verandahs, gawping. When the sun went down, we would go down to the Club, to gawp at each other. Presently we would retire to Chislehurst or West Hampstead and sit gawping at the rain.

But we have lost the knack. A decade of Mrs Thatcher has wiped out the birthright of a millennium. We have become used to scuttling around like sand-crabs, eyes focused on the ground ahead. The language itself has turned against the traditional gawp, hijacked by the dishonest illiteracies of businessmen. We must now be entrepreneurial, thrusting and competitive. We must be self-starters, for all the world like motor cars. We must get out there and chase orders before ascending the high-flying ladder of the cutting edge.

I am even told that you like your reading in short bursts now. Little chunks. Sound bites. Like that. Because you are busy. In a rush. Like to graze. Like cows. A bite here. A bite there. Too much to do. No time to spare. Under pressure. Bollocks. Lazy. Stupid. Finger out. Socks up.

It was not always thus. Time was when an Englishman could happily gawp at a single sentence for an hour at a time. The ideal magazine essay took roughly as long to read as it took your umbrella to dry.

Are we to lose this great heritage? No. It must not be. Let us learn from the sloth. We should regard the last decade as a sort of infancy in which we have been, collectively, falling out of our tree. Now it is time to settle down, choose our branch, let our mouths hang open and our eyes glaze over.

A great example has been under our noses for years; as always, we cannot look to the windbags of Westminster for a lead. Instead we must look to a city which has clung with dedication, in the face of great hardship, to the traditions of gawping. The new MP for Liverpool said he foresaw a great future for his city and he was right. While he spoke, a gawping crowd gawped at him. When a madman began to drivel during the announcement of the results, the Mayor himself simply stood and gawped. Even the police gawped for a while before moving in, slightly shamefacedly, and taking the nutter away.

It is Liverpool to which we must look. Liverpool alone can save us. I suggest that, as soon as possible, the Government should make an investigative outing to see how they do it there. A couple of days' gawping should leave them in no doubt about what they need to know.

41

CLICHES CAN BE true. That's probably why they are clichés. Ask any nanny. They are worse than mothers and never forget, even when their minds go. (Go where? Perhaps through a space-time warp, to a trans-dimensional planet where they suddenly perk up when they get old. 'Uh-oh,' their children say, 'poor old bugger. His mind's come. Better put him in a home.')

I remember Nanny Parkin telling my grandfather that it was wait-and-see pudding when he was at least 80 and she not far behind. She went ga-ga towards the end but it was hard to spot. She still ticked you off but thought you were someone else. Once I asked her how she was.

'Nice little boys don't ask that sort of question, Doctor Keith,' she said.

'Do you know who I am, Parkie?' I said.

'Nice little boys don't ask that sort of question.'

It is, of course, true that some little boys don't ask that sort of question and while they remain startlingly little all their lives, they aren't very nice. The man across the way is like that. Face like a robber's dog and going bald in an unforgiveable way. Keeps regular hours. Has special clothes. He has his being-an-accountant clothes, then when he gets home he puts on his being-at-home clothes, with a horrid jersey. At weekends he puts on weekend clothes, to prove that it's the weekend, and goes to B&Q. Then he comes back and puts on do-it-yourself clothes to do it himself. What he does himself I can't imagine. His house is already a riot of chipboard and yet there are whole forests of the stuff stacked in his garage. The place would go up like a tinderbox, and will, too, if he looks disapprovingly at my womenfolk once more.

But he would probably be glad.

I can picture the scenario. I am standing by the window rubbing Connolly's hide food into my favourite pair of Montana calf ankle-bands, hoping that the bewitching and wiggly Annie from the *Daily Express* showbiz desk will turn up to see her friends next door. Presently she does, falling headlong over the 35,000 volt tripwire I have installed. Mr Baxter (for so I like to think of him) scuttles to his window, says 'Tsk,' and folds his arms. Quick as an observer travelling at or near to the speed of light (or 'c', which, of course, = $\sqrt{(e \div m)}$), I have run down the stairs, lashed my squeaking prey to the doorknocker, torched chez Baxter and am back in my study, oiling my shackle-pins while Annie, stripped, gagged and cleated to the leg of the harpsichord, writhes pitiably. Suddenly a bleat disrupts this mood of agreeable *tendresse*. It is Baxter, trying to laugh. His house has been gutted! Only a shell remains! Joyfully, he hurtles off to Do-It-All to start again. I have done the bugger a favour and it is unbearable. I ask myself what I have done to deserve this and back comes the ghostly reply:

'Nice little boys don't ask that sort of question.' Ho hum. It is horrible to discover that the whole network of lies and evasion foisted upon one in childhood is true after all. I shall probably have to accept that molecules are made up of round plastic balls on wobbly springs and that God will Get Me In The End, just like I have come to realise that One More Won't Do Me Any Harm, and that They Don't Know A Good Thing When It's Staring At Them.

That one is certainly true. Take the Germolene people. Germolene, you may remember, is a pink ointment which your Granny had in her medicine cabinet, and which, along with TCP and Beecham's Powders, formed a pharmacopeia adequate for all crises other than falling into a crucible of molten steel, a common emergency in Newport, where *my* Granny came from, and which was treated seriously, with a trip to the doctor and a bandage.

Once, it was so pre-eminent that it was just known as 'ointment' and everyone thought that that was what Jesus must have smelt of after Mary Magdalene had been at his feet with her little yellow-and-blue tin. Now, people have to have pills instead and go whining to the doctor when their athlete's foot comes back.

The National Trust is launching a range of 'authentic' paints which, with magnificent bravery, they are calling things like 'Elephant's breath', instead of the awful Berni Inn prose of most paint-makers' catalogues.

They wanted to call one colour 'Germolene Pink' but the Germolene people wouldn't have it. So 'Ointment Pink' it is. Another opportunity missed; nor has any cigarette company seized on the news in the *BMJ* that smoking stops you going doolally with Alzheimer's disease. Are they daft? Cosmetic companies trumpet the latest 'scientific discoveries' all over their over-priced products and never mind that you'd do just as well smearing yourself with Germolene. Yet the snout firms, handed a gift like that, do nothing. Where are the campaigns? 'Sweet Afton: If Nanny Had Smoked Them, She'd Have Known You Weren't Your Dad.' 'Benson & Hedges King Size: Since We Started Smoking Them Ourselves, Our Heads Have Bulged Out At The Back And We've Been Able To Sack The Ad Agency.'

Believe me, it's all true. I should know. Beats cosmetics hollow. Hell, *I* smoke like a chimney and I've the brain of a five-year-old.

42

WHAT A GOOD idea. *What* a. Britain's Media Coterie. Absolutely. Just leave the tape recorder running while they talk about themselves . . . yes, yes, I see. And black-and-white shots against a grey background. Oh God yes. Quite the opposite of what Bill Brandt was trying to do, yes, and then of course the exhibition and the book, very much a media, um, *event*. And the tape recorder running all the time . . . oh, is it? Now? What, all this is . . . oh. I see.

What, about myself? Oh nothing to say really, not *really*, I mean one tries to inject a little, shall we say, frivolity, a little *glasnost* into what one must confess has become a rather *jaded* scene, one feels one's flamboyance is more a kind of, shall one say, *service* to *others* rather than an *indulgence* for *oneself*, wouldn't you say? Is that it? Oh. I was waiting for the flash to go off. Oh. Aren't you? Oh.

Yeah well we like groove to the er well you know like er the Sixties an all was, it was, an all, well, we reject that false er naivety with the er and like everything with er rain forests where they have all these like amazing orang wossnames, outangs, they're chopping down the like habitat and it's a statement really like well we say you know it's got to stop, all the Group of Seven stuff is so like hypocritical because it's, it's, er all in the hands of the banks, what about BCCI, like the whole banking establishment knew about that all along, just like the rain forests and that. Oh. I was waiting for the flash to go off. Oh. Aren't you? Oh.

Oh *Gahd* rally no that's *too* terrible oh *Gahd* you're wicked, me? Oh *Gahd* wahl of course I'm *still* with Johnny and, you know, wahl, *paps* it's the Big One but oh gosh wahl he's *rally* passionate and we just, you know, have a rally, rally, great time, does that sound too awful, I mean I don't want to sound like some truly truly *awful* person because of course there's a rally rally *awful* recession but I spose one just rally tries to have, you know, *fun*, I don't see what's wrong with that, do you? Oh. I was waiting for the flash to go off. Oh. Aren't you? Oh.

Look I mean I want you to know I'm doing this under sufferance, right? I mean, Jesus H Christ, the last thing I need is publicity, we've got deals going down right now, Eastern Europe opening up, they've hardly got goddamn home movies let alone vidjoes, nothing, I mean these guys are just *Stone Age*, it's wide open, right? Nintendo, VHS, cable, Jesus H Christ if I was you I wouldn't be standing behind a stinking Hasselblad taking pictures of goddamn media dickheads. I'd get a Handycam, hire me a few goddamn kids off the street, you know, these kids, they sleep rough, you give them 50 quid, scrub them down, set them at each other, I mean we're talking *skin* here, right? We're talking *hard core*, I mean, what'cha think the goddamn Poles would pay for *that*, right? And I don't want you quoting me, OK? Oh. I was waiting for the flash to go off. Oh. Aren't you? Oh.

Talk? About what? You've got all the information you need from my Press agent. Just take the picture, OK? Oh. I was waiting for the flash to go off. Oh. Aren't you? Oh.

What are you going to say about me? I mean, yeah, right, I work for PTFA – Pratt Twat Furbus Abrawang, right? – during the day but I've got this very very exciting project for Channel 4, it's kind of counterpointing heavy metal tracks against a visual montage of promo techniques, I'm talking a lot of *heavy* post-production work, OK, totally investigating a wholly new kind of self-referential visual language, no image like more than two seconds, I was talking to someone whose girlfriend worked with Derek, you know, Jarman, and she said, yeah, she could see Derek being really *heavily* interested in this concept . . . Oh. I was waiting for the flash to go off. Oh. Aren't you? Oh.

You're not going to do some horrible sex job here, are

you? I mean, I am a *very senior executive*. I don't want to look like some bimbo, you know? I mean, I think women get a very bad time. Very. Oh, sure, I enjoy what I've got but sometimes I think what I really want is to just stop and have babies but I am not prepared to define myself as an adjunct to someone else, OK? What really hurts is when these men just treat me like a, you know, *bimbo* when what I want to talk about is, oh, Yugoslavian politics, and they're just looking up my skirt. Sorry? Oh, Montana, actually, I got it in Brown's sale, I thought I ought to get it stitched to my knickers then I needn't worry . . . look, if I cross my legs like this you can . . . Oh. I was waiting for the flash to go off. Oh. Aren't you? Oh.

Yes, well, what can I say? It's hard for everyone. Just getting over the divorce, you know, and then of course my publisher was taken over by some men in suits. Ghastly. Well that set me back *months*. And I was just getting started again when my editor resigned shouting, 'I am not a publisher, I am a woman,' and of course that threw me again. Oh it's awful. I have no *facility* for writing, not what you'd call a *facility* for it. It's all chiselled out, a word at a time. But that's true of all art, I suppose, though I hate labels. Artist. Novelist. They're meaningless, don't you think? Publishing a novel and *being a novelist* are different things. When you . . . Oh. I was waiting for the flash to go off. Oh. Aren't you? Oh.

What? No, guv, I've come to fix your flashgun, and by the way you've left your tape recorder running, flatten the batteries, that will, I'll turn it off for you, there you . . .

43

THIS HAS GOT to stop. It's a question of self-respect, do you see, of constructing a self-image that is compatible with an enduring sense of self-esteem. I know about this because one of my mad women has been to a shrink. 'My problem,' she said, '*apparently*, is that my self-image is not compatible with an enduring sense of self-esteem.'

Well, you can imagine. I nodded and smiled and said 'Yes, I know,' and, 'No, really?' and 'Oh, how *awful* for you,' and then it started to rain and she said 'I just want to be treated like a *person*.' Did I say 'Look, petal, if you want to be treated like a *person*, why not try saying the sort of things a *person* would say, like "Why don't we go in out of the rain?" instead of sitting here looking like the before photo in a Pounteney Clinic advertisement, droning on about your self-image'? No, I did not. But I *thought* it. I thought it *very hard*.

It is time for an end to all this thinking girl's bimbo stuff. No more Mr Nice Guy. I want a butch and virile trade. Man's Work. The trouble is, what *is* Man's Work in an age of videodiscs and shell suits? I suppose I would define Man's Work as anything which enables one to justify one of those lovely £800 Timberland leather field coats and a ginger NuBuck baseball cap, but I may have the wrong attitude. Perhaps Man's Work is where you get a uniform, something sweaty and brutal and deliciously pervaded with institutionalised violence, where causing anguish and suffering to complete strangers is not only legitimate but compulsory.

The trouble is, that would include gang rape (only marginally acceptable as Man's Work) and VAT inspection (not acceptable as anything at all). Once we made a woman VAT inspector run away from the dinner table, crying, but how much nicer would it have been were she one of the ones with testicles, not actually a man because they don't do those in the VAT, but one of those etiolated, low-testosterone ones with a nodding head like a bulb on a stalk, and a thin shirt and composition soles; one of the ones with a mail-order Tie Tidy and a bald spot, with a dirty magazine on the top shelf in the garage (dry little fantasies about replying to the contacts ads, *M44, F37, 34-25-36, she AC/DC, seek similar for sexy evenings, ultimate not essential, into photos, DIY, toys, stockings, cleanliness and discretion expected and assured, Box 3773*) but of course Shirley would never go along with it and who would look after the kiddies, and another thing, what about the ones who *don't* put 'Cleanliness and discretion expected and assured'? Do they wallow, unwashed, in their filth like hogs and tell *everything* to *everybody*? No, best not, although a man may dream, except at work where dreaming is out. (Mr Purgatroyd takes a dim view of dreaming, how would it be if everybody dreamed?) Curious to think that the collection of the State's vicious revenues is in the hands of men who are saving up for a Flymo.

So what does that leave? I suppose there was once a time when it was possible to be a Manly Vicar, but now they are called things like Ken, asserting in thin, mewling Midlands accents that women can be priests, too.

Which leaves the Police. I have always thought it would be thoroughly Manly to be a big, blue, incorruptible policeman. Everything is right about it. The huge shoes are right, and the scratchy uniform is right. The Manly jerseys with epaulettes and elbow pads are right, and all that stuff hanging from the belt in black leather pouches is right, too. There is a magical rightness about the canteen with its smell of coppers and teabags, and a rightness too about the pre-dawn briefings. Manly Policeman breath misting the station yard, the guv'nor droning on in his special police voice. Even the women policemen are right and Manly. The Transit vans, reeking of feet and beans, are right. The whole edifice is perfect.

Even the brutality is right. I would have no problem with the brutality. I would, for my exam, hit Baz Bamigboye, the great big showbiz editor of the *Daily Mail*, in the eye. This would go down well with the police because Mr Bamigboye is a black man, and I would enjoy it a lot because in the late Seventies Mr Bamigboye trod on my hand during a Sophia Loren photo-call and never said sorry. And if he tried to come over all huge with me, my colleagues would cart him off to pokey and no mistake. What could be more Manly?

The only trouble is the laws. In the old days you Nicked Villains but now you have to poke your head through car windows to see if the old ladies in the back are strapped in like the pack of property swindlers, failed barristers and well-oiled tuft-hunters in Parliament want them to be. Soon, policemen will have to check our teeth to see if we have flossed them properly. Ever since the Great Charter of 1215, bores have been making laws. By the turn of the century, all the useful ones had been made, and now all they do is create silly irritations. Can you believe the little man who wants to ban toy rockets? Perhaps it makes him feel that his willy is bigger than it is, but the point is that this is all *terribly* irritating for the Manly Police. When I join up, we'll have a revolution. Our communiqué will go:

1 All existing laws to be repealed.
2 The Manly Police to nick anyone they find a bit iffy.
3 Move along now, sunshine, that's your lot.

See? Utopia is easy when you stop putting your mind to it.

44

THE GUTBUCKET WAS quite sweet in his way but you could tell he hated his wife. It was hardly surprising. She was a winsome and mumsy sort of a piece and I hated having her in the house. Her lips were pursed. Probably everything was pursed . . . except that you couldn't see it under all the C&A frockery, which was a relief.

She was a cupboard woman. They would go into a room, and peer around, and gutbucket would try to think of something to say but couldn't. She, on the other hand, was thinking plenty but saying nothing. Clocking up the cupboard space, though; you could see it in her eyes. Every cupboard meant more room to put things, which in turn meant more things that gutbucket would have to buy, whether he liked it or not.

She said they didn't have any children, not yet, but they were going to try for a family. I caught gutbucket's eye. A friend of mine once looked an emu in the eye in Sydney zoo and suddenly realised that the animal was completely insane, having all the disadvantages of being a bird but not the one thing which made it worthwhile, the ability to fly. Gutbucket's eye was similarly crazed, for similar reasons.

He was the sort of man whom the women's sex magazines tell their readers how to deal with and it had driven him mad.

My instinct was to take him into the kitchen and give him a refreshing glass of Solpadeine, but C&A Junior Miss (not a day under 35, and stringy in the way of women whose youth has been blighted by the opposing demands of 'Candle in the Wind' and Femfresh) would have been peering in my drugs cupboard and working out how many matching sets of mail-order floral saucepans she could fill it with. Instead, I merely said, 'Trying for a family, is it? Well my Mam is from South Wales and she'll tell it's not the try that counts but the bloody conversion, see?'

You could tell she didn't like it, but you could also tell that he did, and that it would give him something to cheer himself up the next time she tried to coax him into getting amorous. God knows how she would go about it. She looked the sort who used to get kittenish but was now getting desperate and I hoped they wouldn't buy this house because it has reasonable memories for me, mostly connected with women, and I would hate to think of them being retrospectively corrupted by anxiously licit coitus on the polycotton sheets.

Yet I was fascinated, too. The future imposed itself on my reluctant brain. He would be sitting in his armchair bulging dozily in front of telly, when there would be a little click and the screen would go blank.

HIM: Oy.

HER: Look. (Opens package from Theatrical Costumier.)

HIM: What's that?

HER: It's a sou'wester.

HIM: No, *that*.

HER: It's a whalebone leg, silly. (Kittenish) I thought we could play Moby Dick.

HIM: Why?

HER: Well, you know, like Charlie and Di, having a second honeymoon. *You* know. (Coaxing) Go on, strap it on . . .

HIM: Pardon me, *pardon me*, but I very much doubt if in fact the Prince of Wales and the Princess of Wales . . .

HER: The Waleses . . .

HIM: Their Royal Highnesses, I would be most surprised to learn that they play Moby as you put it Dick. I would be very much surprised, in point of fact, if they play *anything* Dick.

HER: Look. (Sheds Debenhams quilted 'housecoat' revealing mail-order 'playtime' costume.)

HIM: Have you taken leave of your senses? You look . . .

137

But what can he say? The truth is that she looks like Bernard Matthews' worst nightmare. No . . . Bernard Matthews himself. Bernard Matthews *in drag* – bad drag. 'Bootiful'? Come off it. She feels alluring, feels that he cannot possibly resist, but if he loses his moral grip for a millisecond he'll distract her attention with a handful of millet and wring her neck. Unconscionable, of course, but what can you do?

Eventually they went away, accompanied by the weeny estate agent, only to be succeeded by a goner.

The goner was an ageless young man who sold dog biscuits and wanted to know where the sun shone in the evening. I suppose if you sell dog food you need all the sun you can get. I felt like suggesting he go to Africa, but then he came back with his Mum, who said he'd just got back from Africa and now it was time for him to settle down in a nice place of his own.

It was like the advertisement for the building society – can you remember which one? – where the grim, barking old fart glugs and bubbles at his son's Overland Experience and concludes 'But I know you. One day you will settle down, and find yourself a HOME.'

Dear oh dear. This HOME stuff is a killer. Before you know it, the goner will be kitted up with his own Junior Miss, and they'll be trying for a baby. It'll be dinner parties and barbecues on the balcony like everyone else and 'That was nice, dear', afterwards, and the coaxing smile, and the little stiffy, and the cupboards. Meanwhile I'll be long gone, over the horizon with a six-pack of Solpadeine and the bad yellow-eyed woman. Some people never grow up, eh?

45

SO THEY BIT the dust . . . and the free world duly rejoiced
as only the free world can. Sudden illness stalked the land.
Sudden illness from lead poisoning. Sudden illness from
gravity attacks. Sudden illness from rope-burns . . . The KGB
bastard was pinched and hauled off to chokey, where sweating
low-life thugs will dole him out some cattle-prod. The boss-
man bastard with the shuddering hands and the smashed, grey
face can now look forward to a smashed, grey shuddering life.
The 'Prime Minister' bastard, the flabby fraud with the cheap
sun-glasses and the porcupine hairdo, was kicked out straight
off, and wasn't it lovely to see him puttering back and forth
outside the special junta committee-room, excluded, humiliated and confused, occasionally trying to smile to show he
didn't mind, but succeeding only in showing that he minded
more terribly than he had ever imagined it was possible to
mind anything at all. Hip hip hurrah . . . and if that's what you
believe, why, you probably believed in the last Great Victory
For Democracy, too.

You may remember it. Coca–Cola decided to 're-launch'
their fizzy pop, making it even sweeter than it already was.
The Americans, a nation of children who continue drinking
pop obsessively even into what they describe as 'adulthood',
allegedly raised such a stink that Coca–Cola was forced to
bring back the old style stuff, unaltered, unadulterated, just
as puerile and horrid as before but now somehow surrounded
with a magic halo of incorruptibility and re-named 'Classic
Coke'.

And now we are to have Classic Russia, with No Added
Communism on the tin and a picture of Boris Yeltsin peering
out, all peepy little eyes and pouchy smug truculence, like
Colonel Sanders. For now, he is the Real Thing. But how
many decrees will he have to sign? How many newspapers

will he have to close? How many organisations will he have to outlaw before we say: 'Meet the new boss. Same as the old boss'?

And another thing: who cares? Let's be honest with ourselves. The only reason any of us give a hang about the Soviet Union, or the Federation Of All The Russians, or whatever it is calling itself – 'Classic Coke' will do as well as anything – is because we have spent our lives being afraid that they will blow us to bits. The reason we are pleased that the communists have gone down the pipe is that we think our chances of being vaporised by several gigatons of fissile plutonium have now receded.

That is undoubtedly nice in the short term. But what of the long term? The USSR was a good place to go because there were no advertisements and the women, though fat, were cheap. You could have had one for a pair of Levis and a banana until a few years ago. Now they have put their price up to a hundred dollars in hard currency, and that's just the professionals. As always, the amateurs are much more expensive.

Another nice thing about the inhabitants of the USSR was that they were agreeably spiritual. United in the hatred of their government, unable to appease their itching psyches with retail therapy, they developed the ancient art of conversation. A dinner party in Leningrad would be short on dinner but long on party. You'd probably get no more than a couple of glasses of sparkling Latvian anti-freeze, but you would be among people who had learned to *think* about things.

That will all change. The newly liberated inhabitants of Classic Coke will either fall under the yoke of Boris Yeltsin (have you noticed how all the newsreaders have started sucking up and calling him Barr-eese?) or they will become prosperous. In either case, they will increase the terrors of the earth in a way that no amount of fissile plutonium will.

It is hard to decide whether the flooding of Europe with poor Russians is better or worse than the flooding of Europe with rich ones. The poor ones will wander around with their mouths open, sleeping rough in Piccadilly Circus and the Bois de Boulogne; the rich ones will drive around in big cars with their mouths open, buying everything they can get their hands on.

Businessmen will move into Russia, and there will be nowhere in the world where one may walk without being assaulted from all sides by people selling things. There will be more McDonalds and Kiev High Street will be lined with Virgin Megastores and Toys 'Я' Us and electronic shops selling tacky, Japanese plug-in-and-watch-your-brain-melt narcolepts. It will, in short, be awful.

In these troubled times, it is best to turn our minds to higher things. We must remember that there is still a great nation on earth where the people are not free; where their thoughts and books are censored and their identities and very souls enslaved for the enrichment of their corrupt and stupid political masters.

China? Of course I don't mean China. Who gives a damn about China? Grow up. I mean the United States of America, the only country in the world where people are taught to be proud to call themselves 'consumers'. If you don't believe me, try being poor in America. Try speaking sense on the *Oprah Winfrey Show*. Try electing a good man to Congress.

The people of Classic Coke may have overthrown the man with the whip but the curious lesson, *sub specie aeternitatis*, is that the carrot can be as irksome as the stick . . . and if you want evidence of that, remember that the women of Classic Coke may be expensive, but in the USA, they have priced themselves out of the market. Bad times; bad times indeed.

46

I N THE REARS, since you ask, shortly after dawn. Minding my own business, cup of coffee, browsing through *The Guardian* when everything suddenly went black.

Though it wasn't black so much as queer. Under normal circumstances – if, for example, I had spent the night with a pair of Siamese lap-dancers and had just been reviving myself with a blast of crack and a snort of amyl, when suddenly an enemy had started shouting through the letterbox and simultaneously all the lights had gone out – I would have understood, and kept my *sang-froid*.

As it was, I had spent a blameless night writing lies about the Blessed Virgin Mary, keeping myself alert and desirable with three packets of Lucky Strike filter cigarettes and two cups of Lavazza Black Label every 15 minutes.

Naturally I thought I was going to croak. Going black and queer, heart thumping, left arm numb, unable to raise any interest in Germaine Greer's menopause: all the symptoms of imminent death. My first thought was to rush upstairs and see if there was anyone in my bed, so that I could wake them up and say, 'I'm . . . I'm . . . uhhhh,' and kick the bucket, but then I decided that the sort of person likely to be in my bed at dawn would also be the sort of person who would just say, 'Oh for God's sake, grow up,' and roll over and go back to sleep.

Then I began to feel sorry for myself. 'I could die here,' I thought, 'all alone in the bog, and nobody would care.' I explored this avenue of eschatological self-indulgence for a while and then I suddenly thought of Mr S. J. Mepstead.

I may have mentioned Mr S. J. Mepstead before. Mr S. J. Mepstead works for the Inland Revenue (B) Enforcement Office, Barrington Road, Worthing, West Sussex, and if you don't believe me all you have to do is ring 0903 509 594 and ask to speak to Mr S. J. Mepstead.

Mr S. J. Mepstead is a collector of taxes who wants money from me. I have paid Mr S. J. Mepstead an arm and part of a leg over recent years but that has not been enough for Mr S. J. Mepstead, who decided earlier this year that he wanted everything all at once. This may strike you, as it struck me, as rather an Eighties attitude and not at all in tune with the caring Nineties but things are done differently in Barrington Road, and perhaps Inland Revenue (B) lags a little behind London fashions.

So there I was, convinced that I was about to croak, and yet, although my brain was rapidly closing down all departments, it still had time to think of Mr S. J. Mepstead. The first service message it passed was: if we snuff it, Mr S. J. Mepstead isn't going to see a penny, he'll be furious, the whole of Inland Revenue (B) Enforcement will be humming with outrage, serve him right for sending pompous impertinences through the post.

This, you will agree, is a comforting thought and I was righteously savouring it when another one came through saying: if we croak we won't be able to enjoy his discomfiture, we ought to pull ourselves together, let's crawl upstairs and ring the Da, get some gen, what? What?

The Da was his usual cheerful self. 'Could be a virus,' he said. 'But more likely to be a stroke. You might find you lose the use of your limbs. Let me know if you pull through. Can't stop to chat. Golf.' As he put the telephone down I could hear him whistling to himself in the irritatingly cheerful way of a man who has just seen the prospect of outliving his only son, so I cursed briefly, went to bed and lay there waiting for death.

Death, however, did not claim me but just hung around like a cheap debt-collector, peering through the letterbox without actually having the guts to kick the door down and foreclose.

In my gloomy delirium, I found myself brooding on

the mystery of Mr S. J. Mepstead. My course was clear. He wanted tens of thousands of pounds. I have no thousands of pounds, liquid or otherwise. He had been getting it bit by bit. Now he wanted it all at once. The only option he offered was not having any of it. This seems an odd way of Collecting Taxes but I suppose these chaps are highly trained.

So much for administrative matters. But what of the human side of things? Who, or what, is Mr S. J. Mepstead? What does he look like, if anything? In an extended, if one-sided, correspondence, I have no picture at all of this functionary. Even the Mr (only revealed last week) came as a bit of a shock. I had always imagined S. J. Mepstead to be a woman, one of those bony ones with painful periods and a tubular elastic bandage somewhere about her person. Wouldn't you agree that S. J. are the sort of initials you'd expect someone like that to have? But no. 'Mr' it is.

Does he go home to his wife? Does he tell her what he has done that day? How is his digestion? Does *he* ever go black and queer on the rears? Is there a particular roundabout Mr S. J. Mepstead avoids on his way to Barrington Road?

I need to know all these things as a matter of urgency, before whatever it is I have carries me off. I shall be returning to Mr S. J. Mepstead over the coming weeks but first I must ask for your assistance. If anyone can tell me anything germane about Mr S. J. Mepstead, there's a fiver in it for you. Otherwise, I shall just have to make it up. In a way, the *Making of Mepstead* may turn out to be my finest and last work. I hope I am spared long enough to complete it.

47

I FIND THAT Mr S. J. Mepstead (of, you will recall, the Inland Revenue (B) Enforcement Office, Barrington Road, Worthing, West Sussex) is occupying my thoughts more and more. It is almost like the old song:

Night and day, Mr S. J. Mepstead is the one,
Only Mr S. J. Mepstead beneath the moon and under the sun.

Not that this is some sort of romantic attachment, you understand; not yet, anyway. I could not say with honesty that there's oh such a burning yearning, churning under the hide of me, although, if pressed, I might admit that there's a voice within me keeps repeating 'Mr S. J. Mepstead, Mr S. J. Mepstead, Mr S. J. Mepstead . . .'

It is strange to think that, barely two weeks ago, Mr S. J. Mepstead meant little or nothing to me. He was merely the signatory on a series of impertinent demands for tens of thousands of pounds from the Inland Revenue. If I thought of him at all, it was as a nuisance, a bore, a minute calculus in my fiscal bladder, in short, a functionary.

And then I began, inexplicably, to brood upon him. I realised I knew nothing about this man who was persecuting me. The mind having nothing to grit against, I cast him as a personification of faceless evil, one who would say, 'It is nothing personal,' and never realise that that was the worst thing about it.

I began — and I am ashamed to say it — thoroughly to hate Mr S. J. Mepstead.

But then, as I invented more and more details about Mr S. J. Mepstead, hatred began to turn into love. Not sexual love, of course (though who can tell what course my affections will take: it is not impossible that I may presently feel moved to take the train to Worthing, seek out Mr S. J. Mepstead, and make fervent homosexual advances to him), but more a sort of God-like love. I have begun to regard Mr S. J. Mepstead as my creature. I want to watch over him. I want Worthing to realise what a guest it entertains in its dull little midst.

For Mr S. J. Mepstead is, I am coming to believe, a prince among men. Even his initials, which I felt womanish until a recent writ revealed the majestic style of 'Mr', I now see as having a strange and iridescent glow. They are initials of which Our Lord Himself might be proud.

If I am truly becoming a better man, it is because Mr S. J. Mepstead is focusing my mind on my shortcomings. I picture Mr S. J. Mepstead rising from his bed in the morning. I seem to see him have a wee before going down to breakfast. While he eats his breakfast, just as God worries about the fall of a sparrow, I worry about the fall of egg on to Mr S. J. Mepstead's trousers. I picture him in my mind going to work, and enforcing taxes. Then he comes home. The following day he goes to work and enforces taxes. Then he comes home. After a while, it is the weekend, when Mr S. J. Mepstead enforces no taxes, but Monday morning sees him back at the office enforcing taxes.

It is (as I see it) a life of almost Renaissance richness, the euphuistical balance of public service and private satisfaction, and it makes my own life seem a poor, ramshackle thing. I realise that, while Mr S. J. Mepstead has been leading a life of purpose and dignity, my own existence has been a barren pursuing of jokes and drinks and women and mischief. What taxes have I ever enforced for Her Majesty? What respect do I command in the Inland Revenue, whether (B) or (A) or even (Z). Perhaps there is no Inland Revenue (Z); yet perhaps there would be an Inland Revenue (Z) had I only lived a better life, paid up with a smile, done my bit for enforcement.

Who can say that I might not have even encountered Mr S. J. Mepstead himself, one evening in Barrington Road; a day's taxes meticulously enforced, we might have found ourselves beneath the same tree (I see Barrington Road as lined with plane trees), each smoking a contemplative pipe before wending our way home through the sea-scented air. Perhaps I would have said, 'Pleasant evening,' and Mr S. J. Mepstead would have paused for a while, turning it over in his mind before saying, 'Mmm. What are you smoking?' And we would have discovered that we were both devotees of Skiff mixture and soon we would have been on morning-greeting terms. I would favour the inclination of the head down to the left, while Mr S. J. Mepstead might be more of a looking-over-his spectacles-while-turning-his-palm-parallel-to-the-ground merchant.

But I am cut off from these gentle civilities which give life its purpose. My name is a hissing and a byword among the managers of the Halifax Building Society, because, having no house, I have no mortgage. I am a bad citizen, a tax defaulter, without a pension I do not know what I shall do. I own nothing except a Swiss army knife, an old Leica, a complete set of *Colour Climax* magazine, a Parker 51 and a bottle of Wild Turkey. My life is spent in drinking, writing and aimless travel to peculiar war zones in the company of a beautiful mad woman.

Having created Mr S. J. Mepstead, I now see that it will not do. Perhaps that is how God feels. Perhaps that is why God answers none of our prayers, just like I answer none of Mr S. J. Mepstead's letters.

It is time for a change. I do not yet know what I shall do; but, whatever it is, I know that it will – that it must – involve Mr S. J. Mepstead. I cannot be without him, now.

48

NOW LOOK, DAMN you. I insist that no more calls are made to Mr Mepstead. I mean Mr S. J. Mepstead, of the Inland Revenue. *That* Mr Mepstead. If you know of any other Mr Mepsteads, go ahead and give them hell. They are outside my remit.

People, you see, have been ringing him up and asking him if he exists. Philosophers have been struggling with this question for several millennia, and it is unfair to expect a decent, law-abiding tax enforcer to deal with such a complex matter. They aren't trained for it. It distracts them from tax-enforcing. It wastes their time. You and I may not give a damn if we waste our time or not, but tax enforcers are different. They would *care*. They would look at their monthly salary cheque with a worried frown, wondering whether they should, in all honesty, make a refund to Her Majesty's Inland Revenue. They would lose sleep. Their pleasurable expectation of the index-linked pension would be corrupted by a sense of unworthiness.

Oh look! A pig! Flying past my window as I type. Now there's a thing, eh? But I mean it. Transgress and my vengeance will be swift and sure. I shall write letters to you. I shall refer the matter to higher authority. I shall regret. I shall be disappointed, disturbed and finally most concerned. Eventually I shall have no option but to consider, without further delay. You will be well-advised to. Your only course of action will be. It will be out of my hands.

Isn't this atrocious pomposity absolutely the worst thing? And it gets everywhere. Take the benighted woman whom I was interrogating about orgy etiquette, in particular the form of gang warfare the Germans call *Herrenüberschuss*.

'That's all very well,' she said, 'and quite interesting, but you'd have to give them all time to get hards-on.'

Well I ask you. 'Hards-on', indeed. What's wrong with hard-ons? That's Cheltenham Ladies' College for you all over. Minds like sewers, but they'd rather croak than split an infinitive.

That's the trouble with the British. We're lousy at philosophy, lousy at orgies, but we lead the world in pedantic bushwa. Look at the Royal Bank of Scotland, which bounced a friend's cheque for £5, then wrote - and charged for – a snivelling premenstrual letter claiming that the sneaky little functionary was 'disappointed' that the account in question was £27.50 over the overdraft limit. Never mind that the *reason* it was over the limit was the £30 charge for bouncing the cheque and writing the letter; how about that 'disappointed'? Doesn't it make you want to go after the vicious clerk with an old wooden dibber and a tube of lithium grease? She is *not* disappointed. She doesn't give a hoot. She is a cheap Jill-in-office exerting her authority, and there's an end of it.

And passing upwards through the hierarchy of petty officials and tellers-off, we eventually arrive (glancing *en route* at the imbeciles of British Rail, the sneaks at the VAT and the parliamentary bores and their ground-staff of rubber-soled incompetents) at the majestic office of the Director of Public Prosecutions, arch teller-off, guardian of morality and anything else you would wish to call the DPP of the day. And there we see poor Sir Allan, duped and hamstrung by the ethics upon which he founded his life.

Sir Allan devoted his life to the law and the law got him. Had he realised that much of the accretion of the law is stuff and nonsense, made by hypocrites to protect their own privileges, he might have taken a different path and been able to trawl around King's Cross for a bit of twitch without anyone bothering him. The law is about telling-off and about being 'disappointed' and only in scope and pomp does it differ from the petty depradations of tax officials and bank clerks. What we need is to repeal the old laws and make a new set, acknowledging the preferences of our legislators for whoring, cheating, gluttony and round-the-clock boozing. Burglary, theft, murder and overt fraud would be illegal. Everything else would be in order.

Of course, this would be less expensive to administer and thus taxes would go down. This might mean job cuts in the Inland Revenue. I don't know whether I could live with that; but I am prepared to try, if only for the sake of Sir Allan.

49

WE HAVE HAD in-flight movies and sexual liberation for 30 years now and we've learnt nothing from either. British Airways (it says in my dull copy of the *Independent*) 'believes that first-class passengers have a heightened sensibility'. The average first-class passenger may not be a regular cinema-goer – 'because he is too busy being successful' – but he is 'fairly discerning and would rather see *Cyrano de Bergerac* in an art-house cinema in Chelsea than a blockbuster at the Odeon'. And we still believe that sexual harassment is something men do to women.

Oh dear. We are back to the office again, I think. This is where most first-class passengers come from and where most sexual harassment takes place. Have you seen the sort of people who travel first class on aeroplanes? They would be terrified if they found themselves in an art-house cinema in Chelsea. Art-house cinemas in Chelsea are full of (a) nice young women of the upper-middle class, biding their time until a husband comes along; (b) film-school dickheads yelping about black-and-white tonal values; and (c) dismal middle-aged people without money; the women prinked but wholly lost and gone, the men with pubic hairs on their polo-necked jerseys.

These are not first-class travellers. First-class travellers are the ones with faulty accents and big pens. Some of them are bullies who run their own businesses, shouting from the word go because nobody has ever punched them in the face and taken their money away. These people fulminate about 'arty-farty nonsense' and believe that it is Ideas which are ruining the country. The endless fall of the perambulator down the Odessa Steps in *The Battleship Potemkin* insults their time-is-money credo; far more to their taste, indeed, is Odeon Arnie on the quick-draw, maximum death-per-dollar rampage. Set 'em up, rip 'em apart; that's the way, preferably in Technicolor; that's the stuff that will see Britain right.

The other sort are, of course, the corporate men, the vicious cowards in suits who have indeed created nothing in their lives and cannot comprehend why others might want to. They are the men who want telephones on aeroplanes for shouting at people back at head office, people who want to be just like them. These people do not go to the cinema at all. They couldn't manage to sit still for long enough and the sight, on screen, of people bigger than they are, talking in louder voices and yet often without apparent authority – suits, huge pens, clearly defined positions in the hierarchy – would destroy their perilous self-esteem and render them unfit for consideration.

So much for that and yet we still believe that first-class passengers are people of taste and distinction, as we believe that sexual harassment is something men do to women. Occasionally, perhaps, that is true; sexual harassment is my own stock-in-trade and *raison d'être*. But it's usually the women who start it.

Think of what women like men to wear. Not grey suits, I can tell you; not done-up shirts with watch-your-ass ties. Yet that is what men wear to work. They wear that stuff to work because women don't like it, because men who wear stuff to work that women *do* like would find themselves unpopular. Hmmm, other executives would think. He's wearing clothes that women like. He's probably off having sex at lunchtime. *I* don't have sex. Why, the little bastard! Maybe he's sneaking off to Petts Wood and banging my Shirley!

Now, on the other hand, think of what men like women to wear. Forget all that tabloid mail-order nylon nonsense; that's merely an erection aid for scaffolders with fat nasty wives. I mean the real stuff. Stuff that is beautifully cut to hint at curve of breast and thigh; stuff that slides over other, softer stuff underneath. A Blahnik shoe with a just-so heel; colours to set off the eyes; a susurration of silk at leg-crossing time, the way the buggers do. Stuff to inflame the passions and delight the sense: come on you, lousy, impotent bastards; come on, what's wrong with you? THINK ABOUT IT, DAMN YOU!

See?

And what does your ambitious female would-be first-class traveller wear to work? Exactly that stuff. The woman who shuffles around at home in a pair of condemned and meaty jeans will dress like a mistress or a $1,000 hooker for the office and exert all the sexual charms to go with it: the batted eyelids, the little gestures, the turning of the wrists, the touching of the sleeve. They will do this to get what they want.

One of the things they want is for nobody to mention this at all. Another thing they want is for men to take the blame.

Well to hell with that. Here's the truth. Sexual harassment is what women do to us. What they call sexual harassment is nothing more than a device for castrating a man who responded to the general invitation believing it was for him. It's time we sued them for distracting us and wasting our time. But at least when you see, through the curtain, some hatchet-faced bozo and an Azzedine Alaïa bustier snuggling up next to each other in the first-class section, you can take comfort that they deserve each other utterly.

50

I HAVE BEEN sent off to do an article on how women have changed over the last 20 years, and it's creepy when you think of it. Most of the women I know have aged about 20 years in that time, and yet if you look in their albums ('Johnny, Boko, Tufty and Spike at Verbier – plus MEEEEE, pissed as usual!!!!') their pictures have remained *exactly the same age*.

Spooky! Woooooo! A sort of 'Picture of Doreen Gray', except in reverse. I don't really like to dwell on it, just like I don't like to dwell on the other thing which has happened to women, which is that they have gone howling mad.

For example, I have been brooding about sexual harassment since last week. There's a clear sign of madness for you: the ability to hold two contradictory and utterly irreconcilable views at the same time. View (a) is that it is every woman's birthright to have every man who sets eyes on her want to take her there and then, without ceremony, crushing her masterfully to his manly chest, his hot breath stirring her very vitals, his hands urgent, searching, blah blah blah.

View (b) is that her person is inviolable, precious beyond price, unassailable (except, of course, to the highest bidder) and that any form of recognition that she is or may be worthy of sexual desire is an act of treasonable *lèse-majesté* punishable by gouging, balls being twisted off, injunctions, ruined career and money.

They are, I suppose, like those dreadful aristos who want everyone to be wildly jealous of them but not to mention it. Who was the grim old beezer who turned against someone his son brought home to the stately pile? After the friend had gone, the son said, 'Why were you so unpleasant to him Pop?' 'Bugger him,' said the old sod, 'bloody fellow *noticed me furniture*.'

There aren't enough of that sort left to make it worth dusting off the tumbrils but we could have a rare old bon-fire with the mad women. We could do worse than start with Mme Edith Cresson, France's most unpopular prime minister *ever*, who complained that Englishmen were poofs because they didn't hoot and goggle at her in the street, and has now passed a law making hooting and goggling illegal. I expect the real reason is that her very own Frenchmen weren't hooting and goggling at her either – not because they are poofs but because she's an old bag in a boring Chanel suit – and so she was damned if they were going to hoot and goggle at anyone else.

Here's another one. Last week I had to address a gathering of computer people at one of those rented dinner jacket dos. It was grim, as always. They got turkey and I got the bird, but then some dreadful bimbo came up and served me with a writ for an unpaid bill. 'I think you might find this inter-esting,' she said, 'and I enjoyed your speech.' There she was, tits hanging out, lips painted as garishly as the newly cleaned Sistine Chapel, tittuping on her high heels and smirking and batting her eyelids. Dualism? Hell and damnation, give me the Manichean heresy any day. If she was going to behave like a bailiff she ought to have *looked* like a bailiff (paunch, anorak, damp shoes and a smell of baked beans) and be prepared to be punched in the gut like a bailiff. Instead, what you got was modern woman: a frock-and-froth job designed specifically to give you a hard-on, and a personality designed to tear it out by the roots and throw it across the room.

The ghastly thing was, it almost worked. I found myself gazing at her cleavage and wanting to flatback the woman willy-nilly. I suppose that is a standard male reaction, which must make us as mad as they are.

There's certainly evidence for that view. Looking at the kept women there, whom the men pay to maintain, you'd be hard-pressed to decide which sex to lock up. The women were all barking, but on the other hand they all owned their frocks while the men had rented their tuxedos. What does that say about the men?

What does it say about men that the hard-eyed bastard's boss came over to me and wanted me to smile at him and say, 'Hello,' and said that his emissary was 'only doing her job'? He's supposed to be a businessman and they are supposed to be the essence of male rationality. You can tell that from the way the financial pages of newspapers are written, in that strange, flat, Fifties prose. Yet in reality, businessmen are all mad fantasists who simply haven't got a clue and even distinguished financial commentators are raving mad, with staring eyes and a twitch if Oofy Prosser is anything to go by.

I should stop being disappointed. The answer might be the consolations of religion but the mad women have got hold of that too, claiming that God was the Mother of Christ, as well as Mary. Mad women in dog collars claiming God was a woman? Well, it makes a change from mad men in skirts claiming God was a man.

51

THIS TIME OF year is always hell for us gods. Look at my own case. I merely opened my beak to suggest that something awful should happen to Fat Maxwell and before you can say glug-glug-glug the bugger has croaked and his empire is on the verge of disintegration.

It is tempting to crow. I always asserted that he was a scandalous crook, a bully and a liar, and I have been proved correct. But it would be un-Christian to traduce fat. It would be wrong to suggest (secure in the knowledge that he cannot sue) that he ran a chain of brothels throughout South-East Asia; that he financed the introduction of Aids into the world; that he was a heroin baron; had carnal knowledge of sheep, fish and chameleons; chopped up his enemies and threw them down wells; was a secret agent for the PLO.

It would be wrong, and therefore I cannot do it, and it is all because of the distorted morality which was thrust upon us by a pack of Semites who, thousands of years ago, got it into their heads that the reason they were on earth was that a God had made it specially for them, and therefore that He must have a bit of a pash for them.

We know what happened then. Commandments, no eating shellfish, end of the willy chopped off, compulsory Hebrew lessons and, in due season, Messiahs and testaments.

Well, look at the results. Popes, fish and candles, masses and pogroms, Palestrina, cherubim, carols, Arkansas fundamentalists in yellowing singlets, Swaggart, Carter, Runcie, the divine right of kings, 'O Come All Ye Faithful', wired and twitching magi, the whole truth and nothing but the truth, black-letter Gothic, communion wine, sexual continence, god-children howling for presents, a lovely Parker 51 for the barmitzvah boy, leave yourself alone or you will go to hell, nice girls don't, discalced Carmelites, the hypostatic union, he's chapel but we are church, Widor in F, Stanford in C . . . and Jehovah's Witnesses.

What we need is a new role-model. And I think I may have found it.

There was a time, a couple of weeks ago, when I thought that Fat Maxwell had all the qualities for a suitably mammon-istic totem: mysterious death, obscure origins, long symbolic journey in early life, several changes of identity, *hubris, nemesis* and great big rum tum tum . . . and most of all, a good chance that he would come back to life again, after a bit.

Even when he didn't come back to life, things were not altogether bleak. Fat's remains were interred on a holy hill; we could claim that he had come back to life, although only a few of us had seen him (it's worked before, after all), and presently we could dig up his relics, spirit them away, and announce that he had been taken, body and all, directly to, well, let's leave the theological minutiae for the moment.

Enough to say that, had my plan come off, we could be celebrating Fatmas next year, and to hell with all this fake goodwill. We could get together and spend money we did not have, and shout, and bully, and have great rows, and eat like pigs, and thoroughly disgust everyone who came into contact with us. Just the same as Christmas, in fact, so there wouldn't be much adjustment to be made; but the difference would be that behaviour which is inapposite for Christmas would be wholly appropriate for Fatmas. But that is not what will happen, for I have found a better Messiah.

The man we will apotheose from now on is Mr Peter Lindley, who last week found himself in the dock for allegedly drugging a pair of Jehovah's Witnesses who called at his house while his wife was out one Tuesday morning last winter.

Someone called 'Jeremy' (for the prosecution) claimed that Mr Lindley's response to the Jehovah's Witnesses was to offer them a nice cup of coffee laced with triazalin, and when they became stupefied, to set the older one aside and to indecently assault the younger.

Whether or not Mr Lindley actually did so, I don't know. But the fact that he has been accused by 'Jeremy' of doing so is enough to make him not only a hero but a new Messiah. Just like the old Messiah, it's not so much what he has or has not done that makes him so important, but the fact that his circumstances focus our attention on what ought to be done. There ought to be a Son of God who turns up and makes everything all right, even if it was not Jesus Christ. Similarly, there ought to be someone who stupefies and assaults Jehovah's Witnesses, even if it is not Mr Lindley.

I suspect that the hour has come round, and whether or not Mr Lindley is found guilty or innocent, there will spring up a sect of Lindleians from whom no proselytising fanatics are safe. They think they have it cracked, these people, going round in pairs, smiling, handing out tracts. How wrong they are. We will have them in the comfy chair crunching the heroin-flavoured Hob-Nobs until it's time for whoopeee.

It is the beginning of a new age. Hands together, everyone, trousers down, and put the kettle on to be ready.

52

THIS WEEK I will review 1991. Next week I shall offer you my predictions for the forthcoming . . . no. Bugger it. A mug's game, in my opinion, and this is my column so it's my opinions which count.

Why the hell should I review 1991? Neither you nor I have the remotest idea what happened in it, and we do not care. What is the use of pretending? We have no interest in politics and world events, except as stuff to drivel about at dinner parties to excite the admiration of women with big breasts and the rage of men called things like Norman Dogdeath from Internal Audit, and Dr Bendigo, and Shirley's friend Adrian Whitgift, you must remember Adrian, you know, he writes for *Railway World*, works in valves or possibly siphons, anyway I think you'll like him and for God's sake don't get carried away about Vic Reeves, you know what happened last time.

Which is a pointless exercise. Dogdeath, Whitgift and Bendigo are no more interested in politics than you are. What they really want to talk about is:

1 Money
2 Their operation
3 Their relationships
4 Their feelings

Your best bet is to operate the California Gambit, and immediately launch into an earnest recital about how you had to have this incredibly expensive operation which broke up your relationship and now you are trying to come to terms with your feelings. Be sure to remember that it all goes back to your relationship with your mother, who made you feel that you were only acceptable as long as you continued to come top of the class and scored goals and always had a clean face and shiny shoes and pulled your tassel back every time you had a bath. It is advisable at this point to quote Philip Larkin. You may use a Northern accent if you wish, but be sure to remember that the important line is 'They fuck you up, your mum and dad,' contrary to all human experience which suggests the second line is the one which counts, the one which goes 'They may not mean to, but they do.'

Bendigo, Dogdeath and Whitgift will now be thoroughly irritated, and the skinny blonde with the tic and the hot, toffee-coloured eyes will be feeling enough pity to be convertible into an empathy poke later . . . but how are you going to get through the next three hours? There is the meat to come ('Yes, not bad, is it? I got it at Smithfield this morning, Mariella won't countenance Safeways and I must say Smithfield is fascinating, all those Brueghel faces, have you read that book *Meat* by that French woman, it's about this girl who works in a *boucherie*') and then the pudding ('It's Perdita's grandmama's recipe! The secret's the fresh orange peel!' 'Great!') and then the Drambuie ('Have you seen their commercial?' 'With the actor from – is it *The Terminator*, I think – that one . . .' 'And then the butler drops it!' 'God yes!') and then the coffee by the fire ('It's actually not a coffee pot actually. Alistair brought it back from the Hindu Kush, they make this infusion of rock samphire and cardamom but they don't do rock samphire at Safeway.' 'Or Smithfield ha ha!' 'Ha ha or Smithfield!')

But you have to get through it, so you might as well reminisce about the sort of year you have had. Given that you cannot remember a thing, as aforesaid, about your actual year, I am prepared, as a gesture of seasonal ill-will, to provide you with a year to look back on. Cut it out and take it with you. If you get stuck, you can slip off and read it on the lavatory. No worries, eh?

JANUARY You first started to have some worries about that man John Major. You couldn't sell your house. A pair of Dutch lesbians shunned you on the bus. You believed something you read in GQ magazine but on the other hand your verruca came back. On Wednesday 9th you were going to have lunch with someone but she cancelled. Later in the month you thought the Wigmore Hall was in Kensington, and on the 24th Anthony rang you to say he'd seen a laser.

FEBRUARY Well, frankly, you had been thinking about it and you were glad that miserable mad old bitch was thrown out. You realised she was single-handedly responsible for the mess the country is in, all those estate agents and barrow boys. On the 6th you asked Mr Curtis what the stuff the Chinese call 'seaweed' really is. He didn't know, but did you ever try that Japanese food? Sandy found your briefcase but your Ribena Berry Bunch Musical Money Box still didn't arrive. You couldn't work up much excitement about the Gulf War but frankly anyone with any sense could have seen that Saddam was up to no good. And what about that supergun, eh?

MARCH You read something about shirts in GQ, but didn't agree with it. The verruca lotion seemed to do the trick until the 5th. Perhaps it was the Hush Puppies you bought in Ventnor the summer when you were going out with that Joanna, the one with the wall eye. The gas-filled height extender column on your desk chair went wonky but there was nothing Len could do about it. Funny, you'd forgotten about the wall eye. Abigail Rostrand mentioned a book about Palestrina over coffee. Mr Cassell queried your chitties. Say what you like, Mrs Thatcher was firm, more than could be said of the hooting, wet-lipped so-called 'Government' she left behind. Your house didn't sell.

APRIL Your verrucas went away but your cold sore came back. Some actors and stuff were banging on about Aids and safe sex. You abjured that Melissa from Corporate Communications, even though she was gasping for it. On the 15th you could not recall whether you had told Geoff that you'd had her or not. On the 22nd, somebody rang in tears from the Notre Dame Hotel, Jerusalem, at three in the morning, wanting to speak to Terry Foulkes. You never did find out who Terry Foulkes was.

MAY A woman from St Lucia told you that your lucky furniture was the coffee-table. On the 12th, you wondered who, if anyone, wore Dunhill clothes. Mrs Fellowes had three nose-bleeds in one day. You had a nightmare about Mr Mepstead. On the 28th you decided not to take up Tai Chi Chu'an because you couldn't remember where the apostrophe went.

JUNE A tall, big-nosed man with a red face in Gordes told you he knew how to get to Peter Mayle's house, but you lost your nerve. A clown followed you in Avignon. Your Barclaycard expired in the middle of dinner. On the way home again you shared your *couchette* with a mysterious stranger who crept into bed in the middle of the night with an alluring rustle of silk. In the morning he turned out to be a computer programmer from Maastricht. On the 18th you awoke with what looked like an erection, recession or no recession. Nobody came to view your house while you were away.

JULY Nobody came to view your house, though you were here the whole time. You were going to have dinner with Annelise but she had diarrhoea instead. Someone rang to ask if you'd like to address the IBM Sales Conference in Juan-les-Pins, but it turned out they thought you were Terry Foulkes. You felt it was too early to judge Mr Major's performance, but on the other hand that Francis Maude gave you the willies. Thingummy, what's-his-name, that Mr Cracknell from Reconciliations, he said that Francis Maude gave him the willies, too.

AUGUST Somebody came to view your house but you were in bed with a bug and didn't hear the doorbell. You got a fertilised egg on the 20th. You thought that sort of thing didn't happen any more, what with battery farms and everything. On the 22nd you remembered about the little lion, but couldn't remember whether it was before your time or not. American Express cancelled your card.

SEPTEMBER You wondered if you were going to be made redundant. Dicky Greenstone said it was all the bankers' fault. You said, what about the accountants, then? He agreed. Mr Furtt said he thought those NatWest people had a cheek, they called you in and shouted at you while all the time it was all their fault the country was going down the plug. Thirty quid to bounce a cheque? A bloody liberty. You agreed it was a bloody liberty. Dicky Greenstone agreed it was a bloody liberty. On the 30th, Mr Twiss of NatWest called you in for a chat. You said it was a bloody liberty. He asked you to make alternative banking arrangements.

OCTOBER You had the dog's abscess dealt with. Mrs Stoney's tree finally fell down. On the 17th you had your tooth done. If you had died in the dentist's chair that would have given her something to think about. You read an article in *Cosmopolitan* about how horrible men were. You said, what about women, then? Alan Horowitz from Data Processing agreed.

NOVEMBER They didn't make Jumping Jacks any more. Hadn't for years. Bloody women.

DECEMBER You decided that the recession was well set in. On the 10th you went to Hamleys for your god-daughter's present. You wondered about children. Bloody women. Nobody came to see your house. You were made redundant after all. You told Naomi Bender that things could only get better. She said she should bloody cocoa. Bloody women.

53

APPY NEW ... NO. I am not going through with
this. What is the point? How would you feel if I
waved at you in the street, crying 'Well, hello! Hope
you grow a third leg!' or expressed the wish that your thin and
irritable wife would suddenly say 'Hey, honey, why, don't I
slip into my latex bustier and we can pop off to Paris for an
anything-goes orgy!'?

Quite right. You would say: 'Come off it. Fat chance.'
Fat chance of a happy New Year, too. It will be every bit
as horrid as the old one. And do not think I am being surly
and discouraging. I am not. I just don't care about your New
Year.

My New Year will be fine. There will be rum, parrots,
drugs and schoolgirls, fishnets, Learjets, expeditions and
even, if I am very lucky, a baby rat. My lens-pusher Richard
Caplan has obtained a limited edition Summilux 35mm 1:1.4
Aspherical, and has sold it to my copyright agent, despite the
queues of Singapore millionaires offering him five times list
price, and so I enter 1992 happy in the knowledge that
money cannot always even buy you the sort of stuff that only
money can buy. The bad yellow-eyed woman has thought
up a new perversion involving leg-irons, and by pure chance
I have some leg-irons, so that's all right.

And, best of all, come February, Her Majesty's Inland
Revenue is going to blow its chances of getting any more
money from me at all, ever.

There was a time when I hoped that the dismal functionaries of the Revenue would be called to book for their
mishandling of my case. Had they been polite, they would
have been paid. From the fathomless depths of their collective
insecurities they were pompous and importunate. In consequence they have failed in their duties, and one might have

hoped that they would be fired, would decline and grow ulcers, would become wholly impotent, be spurned, sued, repossessed and evicted, and presently be found wandering around Piccadilly Circus tube station, eating Kiwi Dark Tan from the tin.

But I no longer worry. Just as a man who had been cheated by a Hamburg whore might have ceased to scheme for her downfall in 1939, when it became obvious that the entire city would soon be flattened, so individual tax men and their little erectile problems no longer disturb my sleep.

In the last 12 months, things have changed. The *Zeitgeist* is now rearing monstrously, flapping its wet white sheet, grimacing horribly, shouting 'Wooooo! Woooooo!' and the people who are being shouted at are the men in suits.

For those of us who have been pointing the bone at men in suits for many years, this is a majestic vindication. I feel like a prophet, acknowledged at last. *This is the record of John, when the Jews sent priests and Levites from Jerusalem to ask him: Who art thou? And he confessed, saying plainly, I am not the Christ.* Me neither, but I have been preparing the way, and if anyone wants to set my words for viol consort, six-part choir and countertenor obligato, my agent is open to negotiations.

Because what has happened is that everyone has suddenly turned against the men in suits. We have not yet acquired the Italian trick of simply ignoring them, but we are beginning to regard them with the contempt they so richly deserve.

Look what the last year has given us. It has demonstrated the Stygian incompetence of Mr Major's government. It has revealed the insane and suicidal incompetence of Mr Maxwell's bankers; and what could be more besuited, *fons et origo*, than a banker? It has shown us the snivelling venality, rudeness, and sheer wet-arsed panic of the high street banks, the criminal stupidity of the City, and the fawning, self-regarding, pot-bellied, wet-lipped inadequacy of the suits on the boards of almost every British business.

If the Eighties were the decade when the accountant's suit dazzled us all, the first year of the Nineties showed how flimsy his garments were: tacked up out of cheap shoddy, they split and burst at the first shower of rain, exposing the thin white shanks, the pot belly, and the grey, withered organs of degeneration beneath.

Now his day is done. We won't believe him again. Not when he boasts that it all comes down to prudent management. Not when he tries to sell us a house, or a pension, or shares. Not when he says he is capable of being left in charge. Not ever.

We have now, finally, realised this. And it is time to return the men in suits to their little houses. Let them have a Black and Decker Workmate in the garage, and make things out of chipboard at the weekend. Let them wear special outfits: a blue boiler suit for their chipboard depradations, a Barbour and corduroys to go to Safeway, a Giles Brandreth patterned jumper for when they think they might get a poke from their fat girlfriend. Let them go bald, in that unforgiveably suitish way. Let them wash their balls in Dettol.

But let us never, ever let them be in charge of anything again. And will that help you have a happy New Year? No. For that to happen, we have to kill Janet Street-Porter, the next great Enemy of the People. We could make it look like suicide – slashed to death by her own teeth – but there will still be risks. Any volunteers?

54

ARE YOU ORGANISED? I mean, do you know where things are? Is there a place for everything and is everything in its place? Do you believe that an orderly desk is the sign of an orderly mind? Can you lay your hands on any document without thinking? Do you strain and strain at stool? How many times a month does your wife say, 'Never mind, darling, you're probably just tired'?

It all ties in. There was a horrid quiz in, probably, the *Evening Standard* or possibly the *Sunday Times* about how to Cut Down On Paperwork Paranoia, with blobs and subheads and an Action Plan to follow, but that is all nonsense and you know it. Either you are like my enemy Fennimore from school, with a shiny briefcase and socks pulled up for the rest of your life, or you get laid a lot. It's a question of priority, and I don't mean 'A Priority', 'B Priority', 'Pending', 'Delegate', or any of that weasel-dung they give you on those useless time-management courses where you have to buy a special diary and a computer program as well as paying to listen to a man with a speech impediment tell you how awful he used to be.

Perhaps I should give courses in mismanagement. I could stand on a rostrum with 200 whey-faced executives and tell them how I used to be an organised sort of a chap with a Georgian house, a BMW, a wife, a little family, a gold Amex card and all that stuff, until one day I met a woman in whose eyes was discernible that irresistible fine, rich glint of lunacy, and thereafter everything went to hell.

I could give advice. Fornication, drink, drugs and aeroplanes are the key. To hell with prioritising your work; prioritise your *life*, which means that any insolent nonsense emanating from importunate functionaries goes straight in the rubbish bin, and what's more you don't operate on the principle that if it's important, they'll write again; *that* stuff goes straight in the rubbish bin, too. If it's important enough to warrant your attention, they'll eventually send fat, burping *Auto Express* readers round, dressed as bailiffs, to break in and take away the sofa, and my recommendation (I could say) is to let them get on with it.

Do you think people would pay £235 + VAT for that stuff, hot chicken lunch included? Neither do I, but it would make them a lot happier than Waving Goodbye To The Paperwork Log-jam.

On the other hand, I do yearn for it sometimes. A woman called Silk came round this evening, in high heels and with one of those lower lips you absolutely have to bite just hard enough to draw blood (in my game, you take whatever body fluids you can get) and so I had to tidy up the reeking, whisky-sodden brothel I call my workroom. I Waved Goodbye To My Paperwork Log-jam by putting it all on the doorstep for whatever it is that keeps leaving half-chewed, disturbingly anthropoid bones on the mat.

And, do you know, I was so excited about my clean, tidy desk that I began to believe that I also had a clean, tidy mind, and, what's more, that *that was what I had wanted all along*. I made resolutions. I determined to find the FiloFax my grandfather gave me in 1960, before you were even born. I decided to buy FiloFax paper in eight different colours, and, this time, to work out a coherent scheme for what the colours would represent. I vowed to send out Invoices and Statements, and Keep Accounts, and, in every possible way, to be organised and good.

Then the woman Silk turned up, and, of course, all these noble resolutions were completely forgotten in a sort of testosterone Chernobyl which left me gasping and spluttering inwardly like a beached . . . a beached . . . is there anything which gets beached that is also irresistibly attractive? Because, if not, forget it. Just accept that I forgot about the clean tidy mind and fell headlong back into the old filthy, chaotic one for a good old wallow.

None of it works anyway, unless you are the sort of person who not only always uses a throwaway Bic until it has finally run out, but also has a new one ready and waiting; the sort of person who takes the phrase 'petty cash' seriously; the sort of person who is happy with a woman who never runs out of Harpic but abjures troilism and steak tartare.

Sometimes I wish I were that sort of person but about an hour ago, after the woman Silk had slithered off to her perfumed tropic lair, I fired up a new, smart computer program which someone gave me which claims to Organise My Thoughts. It clearly *would* help, except that I found myself wholly incapable of coming up with any Thoughts for it to Organise. What was worse, I didn't even realise this lamentable inadequacy, because I was sitting there drooling over the woman Silk.

I don't know what all this means, of course. All I can say is that things are more like they used to be than they are now. There's a thought, eh? Now let's see you organise it.

55

WHO WORKS OUT what we are going to be like next? Where do they live? Where do they hold their meetings and who gives them authority? We may not give a fiddler's non-penetrative recreational encounter what they say, but the questions should still be asked.

We know, for example, about the fashion people. There's a special committee which meets in Italy to decide what colour your new clothes will be three years from now. You may think that you decide on the colour of your clothes, according to some arcane 19th-century French theory of colour-music; or perhaps, being British, you long ago decided to settle for grey.

In either case, though, your sense of self-determination and free will is an illusion. You may be looking forward to celebrating your discharge from bankruptcy in 1995 by buying a new shirt, but the colours on offer have already been decided by a pack of self-regarding fruits and harpies in Turin sitting round a table with clipboards.

At least we know who they are. And at least they get it right. If the fruits or harpies say that Ashes of Rose is the lead colourway, you can rail all you like. You can shout, 'No it isn't, I refuse to be dictated to.' You can ask yourself why they think sticking an extra syllable on the end of the word 'colour' turns it into something you need to take professional advice about. But, come 1995, the shops will be full of Ashes of Rose, and the fashion editors will be gushing about the soft autumnal shades matching the softer mood of 1995, accompanied by moody black-and-white pictures by Herbie Knott which give you no idea what Ashes of Rose looks like, or weird and twisted black-and-white pictures by the Douglas Brothers where you cannot even tell which is the bit that *would* be in Ashes of Rose if the picture were colour.

You might at this point get sidetracked by the whole idea of the Douglas Brothers. Why does it take two people to take a snap? When they say that one of them might not be feeling inspired that day, does it imply that the other one *is* inspired? Do they listen to tapes from They Might Be Giants while they work?

Fruitful speculation, I agree, but not the point. The point is, where do the *Zeitgeist* consultants come from? And why have they not been replaced? After all, they are not very good at their job. How often, when all the silly pages of the papers predict in unison a change in our attitude, is it mere afflatus? Think of the Nineties. This was supposed to be a caring decade. It was meant to be the Age of Aquarius. We were all going to wear terribly, terribly soft white sweaters and sit on elaborate sofas, sipping Aqua Libra, listening to elevator music and having beautiful thoughts.

That, at least, was what the *Zeitgeist* consultants told the silly page editors in one of their secret briefings. But the *Zeitgeist* consultants were wrong.

You may think it was the recession. You may have a foolish notion, gleaned from the papers, that all that painful bullshit about crystals and universal peace is a luxury which, now that Government policies have reached fruition, we can no longer afford. You may be one of the hopeful who think we are all postponing the Age of Aquarius until things get better.

You are wrong, of course. The reason the *Zeitgeist* consultants were wrong is that their prescription for This Season's Fashionable Thought – Soft, Stylish and for the New Generation – relied on empathy.

We don't hold with empathy, here. We may suspect that the perpetual 300–ft cloudbase has atrophied our third eye, and so we *can't* do empathy. Nonsense. We can do it perfectly well. Look how good we are at working out how hurt someone must feel and being glad about it. Whose heart did not give a little skip the other day thinking of David Bowie's reaction to the headline which said 'Trapped

172

in Space – Modern-day Major Tom waits in hope.' Didn't you all think that was great? 'Modern-day' eh? Didn't you all think, bet that makes Bowie feel old! On yer frame, Dave! Har har har!

Oh yes – we can do empathy all right. We just choose not to. Once one starts doing empathy with nice middle-class people with decent kitchens and their own skis, one never knows where it will stop, OK? Gosh, it might be empathy with the World's Fattest Man next, waking up in the middle of the night realising how he felt, being so hideous that nobody would ever, *ever* want to go to bed with him. It might be empathy with dreadfully beautiful women; you bet the lads wouldn't like to understand how it felt to have *everyone* wanting to go to bed with you, because you're condemned always to show merely what you look like, not how you feel.

And, worst of all, we might end up empathising with the barbarians at the gates: the working classes, you know, wogs and what-have-you, wetbacks and goddamned Eastern Europeans. That would be the end. The end. Before you knew it, there'd be a recession on. Oh no thank you very much; not for *us*.

56

I AM NOW a man of straw. Everything I own is now to be delivered up to Her Majesty's Inland Revenue. Unfortunately, I own nothing, as I tried to point out long ago, but there you go. Nor is it some fiscal dodge. I simply cannot see the point in having things I don't need.

I am now mobile. Upwardly so, I suppose, since I have now hit rock bottom. 'Rock bottom' sounds nasty, but in fact the whole experience is rather disappointingly painless. The bad yellow-eyed woman made me take my toothbrush in case I got carted off to pokey. She said that the secret of a happy prison life was to submit cheerfully to buggery from morning till night, but phooey to that. I once spent six months as a PR person, and I'm not getting caught twice the same way. Five quid to anyone who gets the extra joke in there. Answers on a postcard to the Official Receiver who now has possession of my estate.

Official Receivers are called things like Dolman, Sibley, Chillery, Norris and Pugh. I wonder if there's someone in Whitehall making up their names. I have not met the one in possession of my estate, and maybe never will, but I like to think of him as a kindly, white-haired old gentleman with a twinkle in his eye and a bag of humbugs for passing children, a man who has seen the troubles of the world but who remains untainted. On the other hand, he might be a she, a six-foot redhead, carnal as Messalina, who Officially Receives dressed in severe fitted bombazine beneath which satin, silk and latex play their susurrant music to torment the newly indigent. I do not know. Perhaps I do not even care; I don't know that, either.

What I do know is that the Da completely missed the point, as usual. The old darling is the intellectual equivalent of a Cruise missile. Every sentence begins, 'The whole point is this,' proceeds doggedly towards the target, then veers off at the last moment and explodes harmlessly in the undergrowth.

It's got worse since he took up golf again. Perhaps the swing sends the blood rushing to his brain and it gets over-enriched and out of kilter. Anyway, he rang up the following day and said, 'Hear you've gone bust. Seems a good idea on the whole, *but whatever you do*, don't go writing about Mr S. J. Mepstead any more or you'll get his back up.' Oh dear. The whole point is in fact that Mr S. J. Mepstead's claws have been drawn, and the condition of his back is now between him and members of the chiropractic profession.

My only regret is that he didn't turn up at court to watch his Pyrrhic victory. I wish he had. I could have told him that he has been elected an honorary member of the Academy Club drinking school run by Oofy Prosser and Stephen Hargrave, in recognition of his services to literature. If anyone still has his number, they can ring him up and tell him so. Second Wednesday of the month. The champagne is on me.

But I don't want any other civil servants turning up. They seem to be a strangely ugly, ill-nourished lot, rather like the subhuman race in *The Time Machine* who lived underground and fed upon the Beautiful People up above. The one who turned up to preside over my fiscal destruction was particularly dismal, a desolately unattractive woman in a pink cardie who looked like a sitting duck for household cleanser advertisements. I bet her kitchen floor is surgically sterile. At the first hearing, she had a gloomy, slit-mouthed sidekick with the worst case of acne I've seen since I gave up computer programming, but this time he wasn't there. Perhaps his face came off. Or perhaps he cheered up and they had to get rid of him.

The incipient bankrupts were almost as bad. They sat along one wall by unspoken consent, like a school dance: a grey-haired man in a grey anorak with a once-brutal face now cowed by misery into a sort of gentleness; an Asian couple, he in a leather jacket, resigned, she pretty and solicitous; another grey-haired man who looked as though defeat was what he was born for; a bearded man with a red scarf, lips twitching as he rehearsed things to say, things which would not help.

It was too late for any of them apart from the Asian couple. They would be all right; the men would not. The registrar was waiting down the corridor with the tools of his trade, an exercise book and a fountain pen, and that would be that.

And the Guinness trial of Roger Seelig was abandoned because he was 'depressed and anxious'. And the new boss of Burton, Laurence Cooklin, has been sacked after 15 months with a £773,000 pay-off, with more to come. And Mr Stephen Dorrell is still Minister of Health. And the sandwich man is now boss of Granada. Thinking of them, I remembered the sad grey men and the sleek lawyers. All I can say is that if Mr Kinnock fancies a bankrupt's vote, he can have mine, and be welcome to it.

57

LAST WEEK'S *EVENING STANDARD* magazine ran a photo competition. You have to send in a picture which represents the Spirit of Disney, and then you win a prize, which I suspect is something deplorable like a trip to Euro-Disney, but I couldn't bear to read any further.

The Spirit of Disney? Piece of cake. Take one grinning bimbo with silicone tits, bleached hair, a full set of dental caps and painful periods. Spray her liberally with intimate deodorant. Pose her on a ruined plinth marked 'culture', holding a fistful of dollars in one hand and a tart on a doily in the other, from which artificial maple syrup drips on to the upturned face of a functionally illiterate 16-year-old in a baseball cap. An intellectual in the background, being beaten to a pulp by a corporate executive, completes the picture.

There once was a time when Disney would just about do. There is, for example, a moment in *Snow White and the Seven Dwarfs* when any sane member of the audience is about to shout 'Mush!' but is forestalled by Grumpy saying precisely the same thing.

But nobody now would shout 'Mush!' in a Disney film. The Executives would not allow it. These are the same Executives who, in their ceaseless pursuit of money, are demanding that we all buy videos of *Fantasia* before they withdraw it for ever, subsequently to re-release it with, some say, a backing track of rap music.

It is not just Disney. My mother bought some Thomas the Tank Engine films for my small nephew to watch, and they, too, are disfigured by a sub-rock sound track. Do these people not see how wholly inappropriate to a gentle, benevolent children's cartoon are the psychotic, brutal, up-your-bum-white-bitch rhythms of ape rock?

I would like to think that it is something that I can lay at the feet of black people but I don't think I can. Black people invented jazz, a genre of infinite structural subtlety requiring a lifetime of dedication to master. Idle, stupid white trash invented rock, because they couldn't hack jazz. Then idle, crafty black trash invented rap, clearly seeing that whitey would buy *anything* if he thought it would annoy his parents.

Now ape music has become the omnipresent anodyne, inducing not a pleasant, dreamy stupor, but a sort of bolshie, stroppy, aimless tumescence.

It is one of the symptoms of the dreadful times in which we live. Mr John Major is another. We are clearly living in the last days, and if they turn out to be the last days of Mr Major too, I shall be only the tiniest bit relieved. Because things are going to get much worse.

In fact, I don't think we have any idea how bad things are going to get. An American historian called something like Derek Hiroshima has published a book called *The End of History and the Last Man* which says that we have seen the triumph of Western liberal democracy and the free market and from now on the great clash of ideologies is over. Well, pooh. What has triumphed is *capitalism*, and that only in the West, and anyone who thinks that liberal democracy is the best political system to exploit the benefits of capitalism is a fool.

Capitalism's natural home is the jungle. You can prove this to yourself by asking a simple question: 'Would I be richer if I were more of a shit?' The answer is, of course, 'Damn right I would.' These shits are the natural end of capitalism, and it is to contain their natural ghastliness that we have invented the ethical and aesthetic system which makes up our culture.

By 'we' I mean the white men of western Europe. We aren't supposed to say so. We are supposed to belittle the white men of western Europe, and to assert that everyone else is just as good if not better, because at least they aren't the white men of western Europe.

But the *truth* (as opposed to the Great Lie of political correctness and joke egalitarianism) is that the white men of western Europe have, for over a thousand years, not only been the good guys, but have been consistently getting better. The white men of western Europe are the flower of humanity, and we are about to throw it all away because, unlike everyone else, we do not wish to give offence.

We have already almost lost part of the battle. EuroDisney on French soil is a shameful moral defeat for the white men of western Europe. It is still not too late, though. We can tell Disney, and all the other insolent, uncivilised American enterprises, to bugger off. Perhaps if we did so we would regain some confidence. Then we could start telling *everyone* to toe the cultural line or bugger off. Loony Islamic fundamentalists, Californian food-faddists, weaselly Japanese money-grubbers, *fatwah*-issuers, wetbacks, savages of all colours, the lot: bugger off. We are right. You are wrong.

This is the Big Issue. Think about it. Ignore what the foolish politicians tell you, and vote on this question alone.

58

I T IS TIME. Time for a change. The whole country knows
that. We. The people. The *ordinary* people. Of this great
country. Have suffered too long from poor government.
And short sentences. And yet. Is there an alternative? A real
one? Or should we all simply give up?

Millions of you have turned to me for guidance. Some of
you have suggested that I should be elected Supreme Ruler.
What nonsense. Elected? Piffle. To hell with *elected*. We've
tried *elected*, and look what we've ended up with. Grey men,
low-brows, cheats, lawyers, tricksters, charlatans, under-
writers, gyps, flimflam men, racketeers, priapists, thugs,
deviates, car salesmen, toadies, cuckolds and windbags. *Balls*
to *elected*. If you want me to be Supreme Ruler, consider it
done. It's up to you. Next time some chalk-white swindler
with a runny nose and a civil service briefcase writes to tick
you off, merely inform him that Bargepole is your master
and you answer to none other.

But if, for form's sake, you wish to pursue the discredited
forms of democracy, here is my manifesto. If it doesn't make
absolute sense to you, you are a fool.

A BRIGHT BRITISH FUTURE
That is exactly the sort of horse shit I will eliminate.
Only a dick head would think a manifesto needs a title. The
future is *not* bright. It is unremittingly dim, and will go on
being so until we drop (a) snivelling PR slogans and (b) the
word 'British', which has become inextricably synonymous
with bad food, cheap dentures, drizzle and chintz.

Therefore, my first act upon assuming power will be to
rename this country 'Fat City,' in honour of Dr Thompson,
who tried the same trick in Aspen, Colorado. It failed then
because the thin, greedy whores and their greedy, bug-eyed

ponces wouldn't have it. The whores and ponces are over here, now, *but we still outnumber them*. This is electorally significant. We can screw them. We can render the place uninhabitable for them. And we shall.

THE ELECTORAL SYSTEM

On achieving power, I shall sack the democratically elected government, the opposition, the giggling white-wristed slickwillies in the middle, and anyone in the House of Lords who got there by political arse-licking, time-serving, bribery or simply sitting there looking like a stuck pig. An immediate second election will be held, at which, to be elected, any Member of Parliament must obtain at least 71 per cent of the vote. Where this does not occur, a Member of Parliament will be selected at random, by a drunken old bag with an electoral roll and a pin. Members elected by vote will be paid £1 per year. Members elected by pin will be paid £500,000 per year.

The first act of this new, reconstituted Parliament will be to confirm me as Supreme Ruler. Its subsequent acts will be of no significance, as the country will be governed by a self-perpetuating oligarchy, itself ruled by me. My Court will consist of Douglas Adams, Little Liz, Nick Mason from Pink Floyd, the bad yellow-eyed woman, Yogi the dealer, my finch Antigone, Hadji from the off-licence, Lovebite, Irma Kurtz and Filthy the Dog. Mr Rory Bremner will impersonate any statesmen that may be required, for example when hosting banquets for mad, sniggering Japanese businessmen. Mr John Langdon will be Court Speechwriter. The Keeper of the Treasury will be Oofy Prosser, who will also be Court Projectionist. 'Lord' Waddington will be Defender of the People, but, just to make sure, he himself will believe his title to be *Prosecutor* of the People. Lord Lane will be Court Whipping-Boy. Paula from the Academy Club will be Supreme Ruler's Perk, fed on buttermilk and kept gloriously naked, save for Manolo Blahnik shoes, opera gloves and a velvet cord around her wrist.

Expenses of the Court will be met by a special tax, levied on anyone who has ever been photographed for the *Financial Times* wearing spectacles and holding either a gold Cross biro or a telephone.

EDUCATION
The future of Fat City depends on the education of its citizens. Until now, generations of politicians have sublimated their nasty urges by manipulating our schools to turn out miserable, docile consumers with blighted lives whose only function is either to do as they are told or be sent to prison.

This must change. With immediate effect, all teachers will be sacked and their jobs advertised nationally. To increase competition, all teachers will be paid £250,000 a year plus unlimited expenses, except for primary school teachers in inner city areas. They will be paid £500,000 a year.

The children of Fat City will be educated on strict Socratic principles. There will be no nonsense about relativism. *Pour encourager les autres*, school governors will be forced to do animal noises on television. Failure to know, for example, what the monkey says ('Eee, eee') or the gorilla ('Ooh ooh') or the llama ('Pftui') will be punished by 50 lashes.

SOCIAL ENGINEERING
We will embark upon a wide-ranging programme to improve the quality of life in Fat City. Orbital mirrors and complex geo-stationary advection systems will be established above the Eastern Atlantic to improve the climate. Mild but effective hallucinogens will be added to the water supply. Quality-controlled Ecstasy will be available from all chemists at a nominal cost. The food 'industry' will be taken under the control of the Court itself and re-staffed with people who are interested in food rather than in money.

We will also address the problems of living in a multi-cultural society by declaring cultural separatism to be silly, childish and an utter wank. The law of blasphemy will be repealed. Anyone who supports the *fatwah* against Mr

Rushdie will be secretly filmed, and the film shown on television, having first been electronically doctored to show the subject apparently reciting the *Credo* in faultless Latin.

Further measures will include a ruling that men must either shave or grow a proper beard, and that nobody is allowed to call themselves 'black' unless they actually *are* black. It will also be compulsory to notice what colour people are and where they come from and to do it with *absolute precision*. This will make the whole thing so complicated that everyone will soon realise it's a mug's game and that it's much better to drop the whole thing and get on with having fun.

THE ROLE OF THE STATE

Far too much nonsense has been talked about the role of the state, and all efforts to limit its interference have been doomed. I will solve this problem in the following way: all civil servants will be renamed 'contemptible lackeys' and forced to be addressed, and announce themselves, as such. I anticipate the immediate resignation of 80 per cent of the current Establishment.

As to the rest of them, minor adjustments in communications technology will serve the purpose. Internal mail, network systems and telephone exchanges will be upgraded, providing an internal communications system unmatched anywhere in the world. At the same time, all *external* communications will be removed. The contemptible lackeys will not notice and can be left to communicate happily among themselves without the rest of us even needing to know they are alive.

BROADCASTING AND THE PRESS

Abuses of press and broadcasting freedom will be curbed. All newspapers and news broadcasts will have to decide how much news there is before they decide how long they will be, rather than, as at present, the other way around. There will be nothing more from Mr Neil Lyndon or indeed any other mid-life wimp suffering from difficulties with girls. There

will be no more stuff about rock music in the *Independent*.
There will be nothing more from Rees–Mogg. *Any* Rees-
Mogg. Nobody will be allowed to take a 'wry', 'sideways'
or 'tongue-in-cheek' look at anything, ever. No more 'funny'
stuff about computers. No more whining BBC stuff about
exploding instant coffee. The Consumers' Association to be
shut down. Playing Kiss FM in supermarkets to be illegal.
That sort of thing.

THE ARTS
To hell with the arts. What do we want with the arts in Fat
City? Give a man cheap drink, loose women and a chance to
get even with his enemies, and you won't hear any whining
about the arts from *him*.

As for architecture, I will, immediately on seizing power,
lock all architects up with Prince Charles for a year. Those
that come out sane will be shot. Those that go mad will be
locked up in the loony bin. It will be good for the people
of Fat City – who needs architects? – and good for Prince
Charles to have something to do now that he is not going to
be King. Did I mention, by the way, that I shall abolish the
monarchy? Well, I shall. There's only room for one Supreme
Ruler in Fat City.

THE ECONOMY
Mostly down to Oofy, this, but a few clear promises won't
do any harm. I shall immediately do something about Mr
Coleridge. Clean him out, I think. Next: corporations. All
McDonald's shops to be nationalised, heavily insured, then
torched. Everything owned by the Japanese to be taken away
from them, pushy little gamboge buggers that they are. All
corporations bigger than they ought to be will have to display
50-foot-high photographs of their directors, naked, outside
all their premises. The Confederation of British Industry and
the Institute of Directors to be amalgamated, humiliated, and
disbanded.

Laws will be passed to abolish retailing. It is a waste
of time. Mail order is the thing. All out-of-town malls can

therefore be dynamited, while the inner-city shops destroy themselves.

FISCAL POLICY

Taxation will be conducted on moral and aesthetic criteria, rather than the current, inequitable system of fiduciary assessment. This means that I, for example, will pay no tax at all, while some sclerotic, hatchet-faced corporate pimp will be taxed into the gutter.

LAW AND ORDER

Hell – with these reforms, who needs law and order? We'll be happy. But just in case, I shall immediately pass an edict declaring that, for any new law passed, 100 old laws must be repealed.

So there you have it. On Polling Day, just write 'BARGEPOLE x' on your paper. Alternatively, simply ignore whatever pack of snivelling narks get 'elected' and, instead, just do what I say. You know it makes sense.

59

THIS RAINSWEPT AIRFIELD in the mad heart of England seems as good a place as any to contemplate my own demise. Half a century ago, youths in Wellington bombers flew out to deal death and have it dealt to them in return; now the American F-111s roar overhead, and, from time to time, a plume of orange flame and a cloud of smoke appear on the horizon to remind us all that dishing it out and taking it are widely differing talents.

I have been dishing it out for a number of years on this page, and now it is my turn to take it. How does it feel? Piece of cake. No sweat. Frankly, it's you I worry about. This week you will vote for the next government, and I shall not be around to ventilate, on your behalf, your righteous rage at the disgusting results of your electoral behaviour. I shall be gone, but you will have to live with the consequences, and no more passing off my stuff as your own at the office.

I worry about you; yes I do. How will you manage? The parade of lunacy and corruption will continue, but all you will be able to do is go red in the face, mobilise glycogen from your under-used body, build up huge deposits of cholesterol in your coronary arteries, and eventually explode, collapse and croak. I wish, like Arthur or King Stephen, I could tell you that I will return when the hour comes round again; that, one day in the future, some public relations executive, some politician or health fascist, some snivelling egalitarian with dandruff in his eyebrows, some stunted corporatist with a filthy mind will go too far, and with a bright flash, a smell of freshly oiled leather and the sound of a celestial whip cracking, I will once more be among you, eyes blazing, tongue wagging away nineteen to the dozen, and in my bronzed and muscular arms a lovely cornucopia of drugs, women and vulgar abuse.

But I cannot. I cannot make such a promise. Why, even the Executives – clever men, *ambitious* men, men keen to get on, with briefcases full of management accounts and demographics – cannot make such a promise.

So you are on your own from now, and serves you right. All I can do is offer you a little advice. I don't see why the hell I should, but here goes.

1. We live in filthy times, and if you find yourself in tune with the *Zeitgeist* you will know you are doing something wrong. Other symptoms of a life coming off the rails include smarmy phone calls from your bank manager, ownership of any item from the Innovations catalogue, nodding in agreement as you read the *Daily Mail*, saying 'Thank you' after sex, and actually quite liking that Jonathan Ross. Symptoms of a life securely established include heavy drinking, constant sexual harassment, contumely, hospitalisation, bankruptcy and death. If you have a nice circle of friends, professional people mostly, one of them is actually a judge – a *judge*! – then there is no cure and you must kill yourself.

2. Do not go to EuroDisney, or patronise anywhere or anything with a capital letter in the middle of its name.

3. If you work for a company which insists that you drive a particular brand of car, resign, first writing off the car in an accident in which two teenage hookers and a hallucinating macaw reach an untimely end.

4. Keep your dirty hands off any woman whose name has been mentioned in this column, or it will go worse for you.

5. If the pressure becomes unbearable, take up a hobby, but make sure it is a suitable one. Unsuitable hobbies include philately, railway archaeology, home computing, golf or anything which has a magazine devoted to it. Suitable hobbies include merchant banking, astrophysics, gynaecology, pyrotechnics and troilism.

6. Make sure that your dress fits your station in life. There is no station in life for which grey Clark's slip-on shoes are appropriate, unless it is that of a junior regional sales executive for a white goods chain-store.

7. Express your anger. It hardly matters what you are angry *about*, so long as you convey clearly the message that you are on the point of a serious psychotic meltdown and anyone getting in your way is liable to be no more than a bag of pimply skin and boneshards lying in a pool of blood within seconds. If you cannot think of anything to be angry about, you need help. For God's sake, are you living in a *hole* or something? Sources of anger are all around you. The climate. The licensing laws. Mr Major. Mr Kinnock. Television cissies. 'Male interest' magazines. The man who invented foil-embossed paperback covers. Accurist's sponsorship of the speaking clock. Marketing men. Aids activists. The man who truncated the glorious French litany – '*Cette sauce . . .*' – on the HP bottle. Architects. Designers of cigarette lighters. European federasts. Sniggering coppers on the Vice Squad. People who say 'I think you'll like it' as they give you something horrible to eat or drink, cow's rumen in bilberry vinegar, say, or that coconut liqueur that the local peasants use to salve their verrucas. Women who ask if you'll respect them in the morning when you don't even respect them now. The people who closed down *Punch*. Use your imagination.

Because now you really *are* on your own. This is it: the last words on the last page of the last issue of *Punch*. It's a privilege; I'd say more, but I would only be cut for the usual reason, lack of